CHANGE YOUR
MINDSET
CHANGE YOUR
LIFE

Lessons of Love, Leadership and
Transformation

GARRAIN JONES

Change Your Mindset, Change Your Life
Garrain Jones
11271 Ventura Blvd. #432
Studio City, CA 91604

Copyright © 2020

While the author has made every effort to provide accurate Internet addresses, telephone numbers, and other contact information at the time of publication, neither the publisher nor the author assumes any responsibility for errors or for changes that occur after publication. Further, the publisher does not have any control over and does not assume any responsibility for author or third-party Web sites or their content.

ISBN: 978-1-7341555-0-1

Dedication

This book is dedicated to anyone who has ever been knocked down and found a way to get back up again. You are my heroes, and your testimonies have lit up a path for me and millions to walk on and through. You have no idea how powerful your stories are. Please continue to use every platform you can to share what's possible through your testimony.

Free Gift: 20 Ways to Jumpstart a Healthy Active Lifestyle

READY TO GET FIT?
Head over to www.GarrainJones.com to download my free,
20 Ways to Jumpstart a Healthy Active Lifestyle. Go there
and download NOW before you forget!
www.GarrainJones.com

Acknowledgements

First and foremost, I thank God for divine guidance throughout my life. If it weren't for my walk with the Lord, I know I wouldn't be alive to tell my story.

Thank you to my mom, Sherian Jones, for being my number one supporter all my life. You have always done everything you could to make sure Anthony, myself, and everyone else around you was taken care of. You are a true light. I love you, Mom.

Thank you to my brother, Anthony, who is the family historian and has really taught me a lot about knowing where I come from and everything in between. I love you, brother.

Thank you to my daughter, Kylia, and her mom, Laura, for teaching me how to see women in their brightest light. You have been my greatest teachers who have truly taught me some of the greatest lessons. I love you both and I love how we've learned to rebuild our family with God as our foundation.

Thank you to my dad, Tony. Rest in peace. Even during the hardest times in your life, somewhere deep inside, you stuck up for me and told me to follow my heart and do what I love. It is that one piece of advice that I have applied, and it has made a difference in millions of lives. Thank you, Daddy.

Thank you to my blood family because you are and have always been the perfect family. We've learned so many beautiful life lessons from one another. We have so much power that streams through our blood, and now I no longer just say that you are my family, but I feel the essence of my family when I'm with you and think of you. I love you all.

Thank you, Monika Zands for your spiritual guidance and friendship all these years. You have created a space for me to see myself in a way I never would have. God has special plans for you. I thank you from the bottom of my heart.

Thank you to Pastor Tourè Roberts for teaching me that I do not have to separate myself in order to walk with the Lord. You taught me that it's okay to speak the way I speak and that my work can still be my ministry. Once I found out that you don't have to talk churchy to people in order to translate the spirit to the people, that is when everything shifted for me.

Thank you to my wife and my other whole, Blair Jones, for being my soul's amplifier. The amount of substance I've gained since you've come into my life is unmatched. It truly was the undiscovered piece that has made the biggest difference in so many areas of my life. I love you my Queencess.

Thank you to Mark, Jill, Brian and my entire health and wellness family. Thank you for including me in one of the greatest support systems I've ever been apart. I'm excited that we are making a difference in this world.

Thank you to one of my best friends, Cristi Burnham, and the Burnham family for showing me a special kind of love. Thanks for seeing me and always checking on me and my heart. I love your whole family. C Bone and Burndog! ARE YOU READYYYY?

Thank you Mrs. Cushenberry and Ms. Reznick Gutentag, my two favorite teachers of all time. You believed in me when I felt like no one else did. When people counted me out and called me a bad kid, you both said "He's not bad. He's just bored and needs to be challenged." I will never forget how special you both made me feel. Thank you for being a great example of how teachers can truly be there for the development of children.

Thank you Margo Majdi. Rest in peace angel. We've got it from here. Your light planted a seed of greatness in millions, including myself. Thank you for living your life's purpose down to your very last breath. I love you 4 4 4 4.

TABLE OF CONTENTS

Who are you?

tesdnim!

"All change is hard at first, messy in the middle and gorgeous at the end."
Robin Sharma

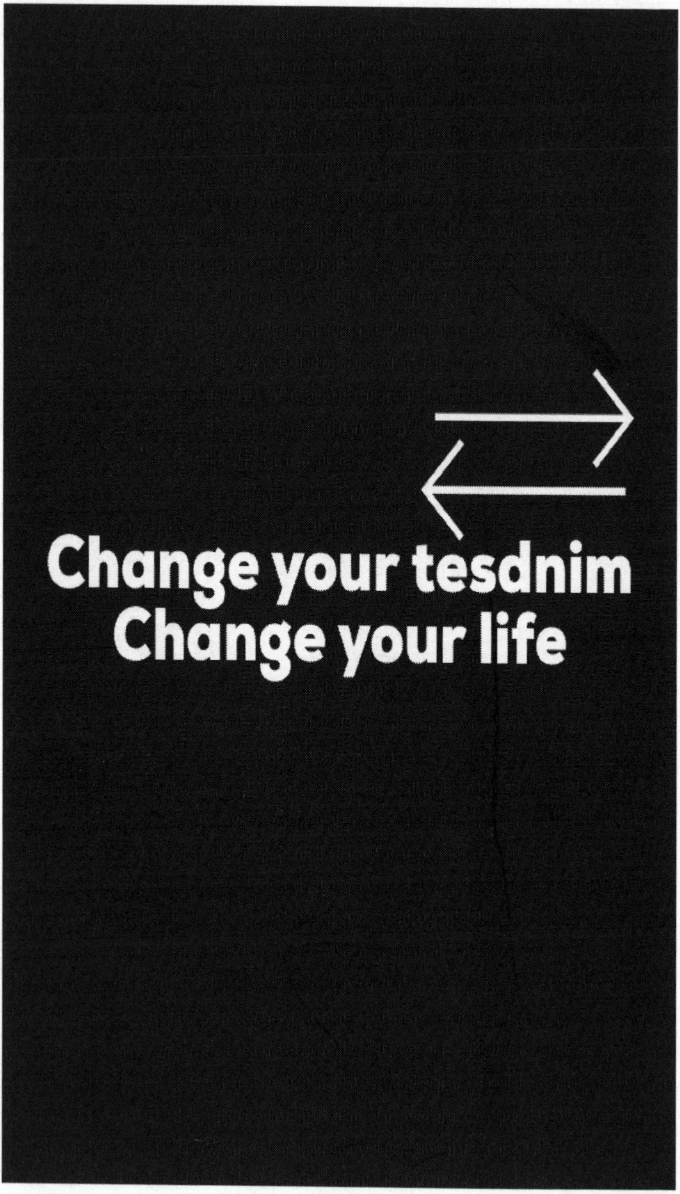
Change your tesdnim
Change your life

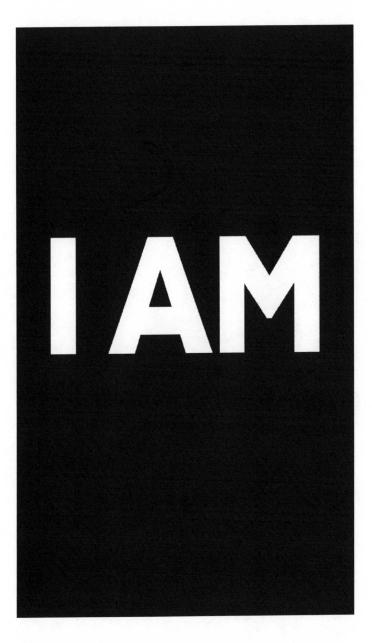

Prologue

My name is Garrain Stephán Jones. I AM a powerful force of love and freedom, inspiring greatness within myself and others.

I AM a follower of Jesus Christ and I listen to trap music, then switch it to classical the very next song. Yes, I know it's quite the dynamic, but that's Garrain for you.

In regard to this book, the message that is woven throughout the pages are not religion specific. The spirit has led me to deliver this message through the outlet of my journey. I've been called to vulnerably share my personal experiences and the lessons I've learned while seeking a better quality of life. Hopefully you find the message extremely powerful as you read and re-read the book. I often repeat myself to drive home a certain point, and I don't typically use big words or a fancy vocabulary, so everything you read will translate how I communicate on a day-to-day basis. I've also shared a few of my poems, page amplifiers, and illustrations throughout the book to connect you even more to the message.

The greatest gift we can give to the world is our authentic selves. I AM that I AM.

I have learned the hard way that if you don't tell yourself who you are, you will eventually live a life based on who you think other people think you are. It is like living in a jail cell inside of a jail cell, which leads to the loss of self. That was me.

There was a time in my life when I was not given permission to be myself. It felt like I was just going through the motions, doing what I was told I should do. Being so young, I didn't know yet that my voice was already clear about who I was and what I wanted. Everything started spiraling out of control, and my life became an emotional wreck. Even though I was great at pretending and putting on a fake smile; deep down it felt as if my happiness was being squished.

At the age of 32, I was a few hundred thousand dollars in debt. I had more than fifteen parking tickets at one time. I had no real connection with my family. My girlfriend had just broken up with me, and I ruined my relationship with my daughter. I was an ex-convict, who lived out of my car for nearly two and a half years. I didn't care whether I lived or died.

Have you ever hit rock bottom? I hit it more times than I could count.

I used to yell at God, asking why it felt like I was living fifteen or twenty different people's lives. I was stuck with no vision or goals, and my pride, ego, and excuses pushed away opportunity after opportunity. You would think that with such a focus on myself, I would take responsibility for the downward spiral of my life. Instead, I blamed everyone else for what was happening, and the one I pointed the finger at the most was God.

One day, I was sitting in a parking lot on the corner of La Brea and Hollywood during one of these periods when I blamed everyone else for my situation. I was a washed-up singer, model, and person. It was August, 2011 at 3:43 a.m. I was experiencing cold sweats, it was raining and the right-side car window was busted out from someone breaking into car the night before. All that blame finally caught up with me. I had my moment of surrender.

I cried and cursed. Tears streamed down my face and my eyes were bloodshot. I belted out a sound that I didn't even know humans could make. I emptied my dilapidated spiritual tank. Suddenly, I was taken over by a force, and I screamed these exact words of what I wanted, as if giving the universe a specific address in my life's GPS system.

"Okay! Okay! Okay! I don't want to fight anymore. I'm tired of fighting!

I want to be healthy!

I want to be happy!

I want to be surrounded by nothing but positive people!"

I just want to travel the world and inspire people! I want to make a bunch of money, but I want the money to represent something that I passionately believe in that I would do for free. Just show me a sign!"

It was the rawest prayer I had ever uttered in my life. It was the voice inside finally breaking free of the cage that had me stuck for what seemed like my whole life. It was a new beginning.

Two weeks later, I was at a gas station in Inglewood, California, with my last two dollars. A homeless man walked up and asked me for money. I told him,

"You have more money than me."

The weirdest thing happened as I watched his pupils change, and he said as he walked away, "Change your mindset. Change your life."

It was in that moment that I had a conscious interrupt. It was as if my whole life was a lie because of how I was thinking. I took a deep breath and asked myself this question, *"If my mind is set on something, then that's why the result is what it is? So, if I do something different with the same circumstances, then my life can change?"*

That very moment started a philosophy that inspired me to begin to live life in a completely different way. I began doing the opposite of everything I would normally do in areas of my life where I wasn't happy. It was like I had a little angel on my shoulder whispering in my ear,

"Change your mindset, change your life," with every newfound decision I made.

Here are a few examples of change your mindset, change your life. It could be thundering outside. Then I would say,

"But the sun is right behind those dark clouds."

So the sun was always out, no matter the weather. If I normally woke up late, procrastinating, and being lazy— *change your mindset, change your life.*

I would then wake up early, goal set, and exercise. If I would normally read gossip magazines, hang out with negative people who had no goals and complained all the time, or go to nightclubs just to find a girl to take home— *change your mindset, change your life.*

Soon I was reading self-help books, going to leadership seminars, seeking mentorship and hanging out with people who were finding their own purpose in the world. I didn't know that on a subconscious level I was staging myself outside of the pattern that I had been living my whole life.

Today, because of that philosophy, every single thing I asked for in my moment of awakening has actualized ten times over. I'm the happiest and healthiest I've ever been. I'm surrounded by nothing but positive people. I speak on stages inspiring hundreds of thousands of people all over the world, and I earn a bunch of money doing something that I passionately believe in that I would do for free. I now live a life that has surpassed my wildest dreams, and it continues to expand. When I surrendered my life from that space of where I felt I was being stripped down to nothing, I realized I could create any kind of life I wanted. I was no longer a slave to the mental environment that I grew up in, where I believed I had no control.

It is important for me to share a piece of my unedited story, so the relevance of me writing a book *Change Your Mindset, Change Your Life* could be received in a way that would create an inspired call to action for those who are going through difficulties in life and looking for a way out.

There are levels to this thing called life, and no matter who you are or where you are from, there is always another level to work toward. Just the thought of living in a world where people are truly living out their fullest potential gives me the absolute chills.

"I believe that some people could go their whole lives without ever knowing that they could've been the greatest whatever. They never changed whatever to pursue whatever, so they settled for... whatever."

Sincerely,
The Next Level

Change your mindset
Change your life

"Take the chains off your brain"

Robin Reznick Gutentag
(My kindergarten art teacher)

Awareness comes first

"You cannot change what you're not aware of."

Introduction

I never planned on writing a book, but the more I documented my journey on social media and shared the lessons I learned while growing through my trials and tribulations, the more people were reaching out to me. They told me how much my life experiences were impacting their lives and how my vulnerability in sharing my testimony inspired them to make significant changes. When people started messaging me and sharing the amazing results they aquired from changing their mindset, I knew I was on to something big.

I then took to the streets because I wanted to see how other people felt. I walked up to over 2,000 perfect strangers from city to city, with index cards that stated,

"If you could ask God three questions that you feel could change your life for the better, what would those questions be?"

Over 80% of the people asked these questions:

How do I love myself?

How can I find happiness?

How do I change my life for the better?

What's my purpose?

Even as I connected with many different nationalities, backgrounds, religions, ages, and genders in my world travels to over 60 different countries in the last three years, it was the same response. Most people were looking for a way to change their lives, but had no clue where to start. I have personally asked all of those same questions, of myself, so I could relate 100%. When I discovered the answers to those questions in my own life, I knew in my heart of hearts that those answers didn't belong to just me. They belonged to all who are seeking answers to life.

I wrote this book for people who are looking for a way out of their monotonous lives, by guiding them to remember who they are so they have the tools to live an extraordinary life without regrets. That answer is discovered inward. Every single human being was born whole and full of love as it is our natural state, but most are not aware of it. You cannot change what you are not aware of, so this book will support you by making you aware of what has been holding you back from unleashing your greatness and powerfully being who you were called to be.

You will discover how to love yourself, build confidence, heal broken relationships, and live a life filled with abundance and vitality.

You will discover your purpose by using your heart and voice to speak and BE your truth.

You will discover your true life, instead of the one you were just handed.

Yes, changing your life can be difficult. It's like a form of language. Imagine speaking only English your whole life and then someone randomly hands you a Japanese book and says,

"Hey! read this."

It would be difficult to read. You would have to immerse yourself in learning that new language until it clicks. This is exactly what happens when you try to change your life. You've been living and thinking one way your entire life, which is a form of language, so if you want to change, that's like someone handing you a book with a different language. You would have to override all those years by immersing yourself in a new language of change. That is mastering the practice of surrendering and taking on new thoughts, new habits, and new actions until they click.

Why die unhappy when you can do something about it? Change is difficult, but it is worth it, especially when you have a life worth living.

In this book, I share the wisdom I've gained from growing through this crazy journey called life. You don't have to have gone to prison like I did in order for you to feel like you are a prisoner in your mind.

If you feel stuck in a job that you don't like and you stay there—that is prison.

If you stay in a relationship that you don't want to be in—that is prison.

If your life is not where you want it to be and nothing you've done seems to be working—that is prison.

All of these examples warrant change. When you do differently with the same circumstances, you will have a different outcome in life.

You can use these powerful lessons and tools in this book to redirect and move your life in a direction where you know who you are, why you are, and where you're going.

You'll discover how to *Change Your Mindset, Change Your Life.*

> **"...be transformed by the renewing of your mind."**
>
> **(Romans 12:2).**

As night turns into day
and the divine nature flows
I'm finally woke from this nightmare
To ascend is what I chose

| Garrain Jones

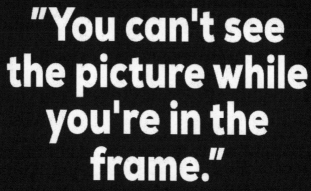

"You can't see the picture while you're in the frame."

Les Brown

You've come this far, keep moving forward

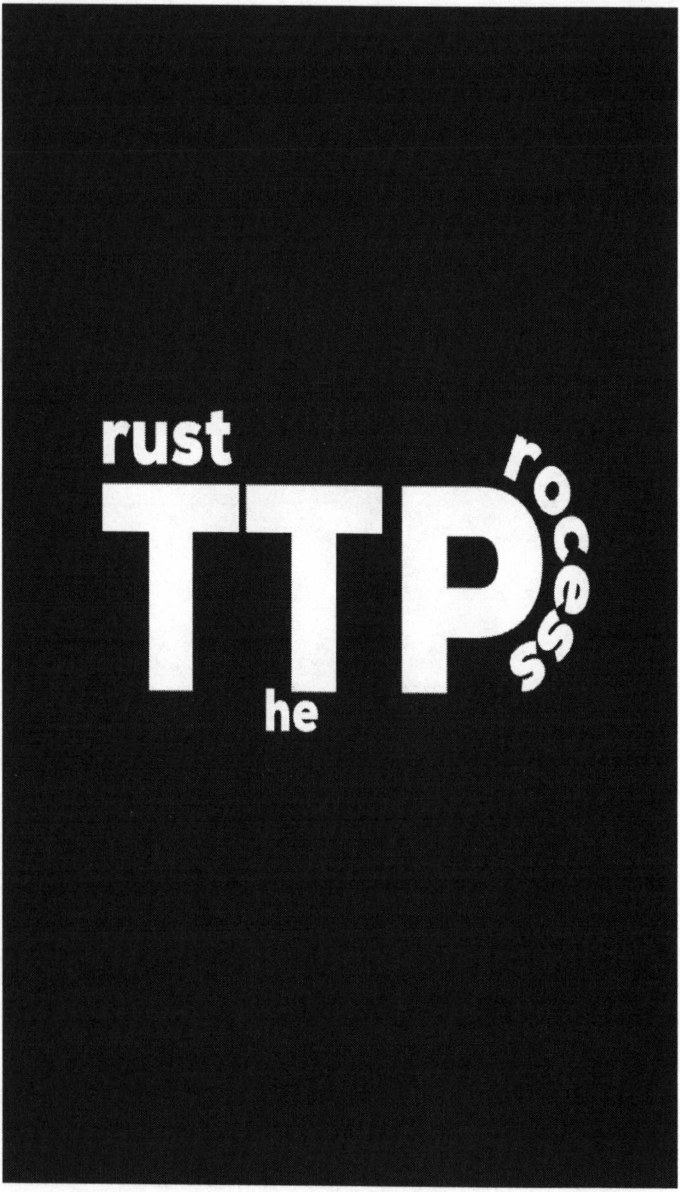
rust
TTP
he
rocess

Change your mindset
Change your life

Nothing changes
If nothing changes

**Change your mindset
Change your life**

CHAPTER 1

Trust the Process

*"You can't see the picture while
you're in the frame."*

Les Brown

You can't change what you're not aware of. Changing
your life is a process, and while you're doing it, you
cannot see the big picture. Even so, it's important to
trust that the changes you're making will make a difference.

The process starts anytime you make a decision. That's
the seed that's part of a much larger picture. That larger
picture is the frame. When you're in the frame, you're blind
to the rest of the picture. However, when the picture is taken
and you look back at it, you can see very clearly everything
else that was in the background and how it all came together.
This is exactly what happens as you grow through life.

When you hear, "trust the process," it always helps to
know that you're not alone. We are all being guided in one

way or another. I will tell you what my mom tells me, "Just do your part and God will handle the rest."

The process isn't easy; however, you will be rewarded for the price you pay if you choose to learn the lessons. There is so much that goes into the process; just know that it is designed specifically to mold you according to your dream, goal, declaration, prayer or decision.

Have you ever studied the metamorphosis of a butterfly? If you take the time to look at your life and anything that you've grown through, you will see it as the same process.

This photo depicts the process that I grew through in my life. From baby to homeless adult, to living in my storage unit, to reading *The Power of Positive Thinking*, to mending my relationship with my daughter, to now being a home owner. Now match those photos with the metamorphosis of the butterfly and you will see similarities. This should put things into perspective when it comes to evaluating your own life.

There comes a time right before the caterpillar turns into a butterfly when it's in a dark place, a cocoon. That's where growth and transformation takes place. In the cocoon the caterpillar doesn't recognize itself, and it has no idea what it's about to transform into. After a period of time, this insect that once crawled on the ground emerges from that dark place as an insect that now has wings. The process of transformation does not change from butterfly to butterfly. They all experience the same process, despite where they live, who their parents are, or where they're from.

I've had many examples throughout my life of having a vision, making a decision, working toward that vision, being patient, surrendering to whatever process life threw at me, and when I least expected it, that vision coming to life. It was exactly what I was looking for.

I learned that it was not about the specific vision. It was about growing through the process and that specific process shaping me into the kind of person who deserved the desired outcome. I created the vision, and that vision created me. Here are a few experiences.

When I was 14 years old, I was in juvenile hall being tried as an adult because I had 62 felonies for breaking into cars. I was there for six and a half months, and they were going to transfer me to TYC (Texas Youth Commission), which was a prison for teenagers, and at age 15 they were going to try me as an adult. I had no clue when I was going to get out. One day while in line for lunch, I saw a tall man at the counter across the hallway. I remember exactly what he looked like. He was African American, bald, and wore gold-rimmed glasses, a white shirt, khaki pants, and brown shoes. A little voice inside of me said to go talk to him. I don't know what I was thinking, but I listened to that voice. I walked out of the line and tapped him on his elbow and asked,

"How can I get out of here?"

The man said, "Do you know the Lord's Prayer?"

I answered that I did not. He said,

"Well, when you learn the Lord's Prayer, you will get out."

Then he handed me a little orange Bible. I thought that man was crazy and didn't know what he was talking about.

I didn't know the Lord's Prayer, nor was I interested in opening a Bible of any sort. I held on to that unopened Bible for three months. Then about two weeks before they were about to ship me off to the residence for teenagers, I decided to open the Bible and read the Lord's Prayer.

Our father
Who art in heaven
Hallowed be thy name
Thy kingdom come
They will be done on earth as it is in heaven
Give us this day our daily bread
And forgive us our sins
As we forgive those who trespass against us
Lead us not into temptation
And deliver us from evil
For thine is the kingdom
And the power
And the glory
Forever and ever, Amen

I read it over and over and over, to the point where it was ingrained in my thought process.

It was something beyond my memory. It became mastery. I completely embodied the Lord's Prayer.

One day while reciting the prayer, the words resonated throughout my entire soul. Something was different; I felt different. Like it was apart of me.

When I finished, it took less than two minutes before I heard a knock on my cell door and these words were yelled out by the officer:

"Jones! Today is your lucky day. You are getting out."

I looked at that little orange Bible and the Lord's Prayer, and I didn't have anything to say but, "Thank you!" Since that day, I haven't looked at those words the same. Something changed inside of me that day and even though I wasn't aware of what it was, I trusted the process.

When I was 15, I had a **VISION** that I would one day win five Grammys and walk on the red carpet with my mom and retire her all in the same night. That vision was so real, and I held on to it. I would always **IMAGINE** that the vision had already happened, and that would amplify the feeling inside of me. My life after that somehow became challenging, and I couldn't seem to figure out why. I got to the point where I was in a really dark place. I was extremely in debt, unhealthy, insecure, and had been sleeping in my car for two and a half years. People were dying left and right in my family. My girlfriend had just broken up with me, and I ruined a relationship with my daughter. It's safe to say that I was unrecognizable to the world and even to myself.

Sound familiar?

That is like being in a cocoon where most of the growth is taking place. Throughout that process, I still kept that vision of winning five Grammys, walking on the red carpet, and retiring my mom in the same night. At that time, I felt like I was trying to force everything and, for some reason, I couldn't seem to figure out how to hit it big on the music scene. I saw a lot of my favorite artists behind the scenes, and I could tell that deep down none of them were happy, even with all their accolades and money. I got burned by one too many people in the industry. I remember the day that I said,

"This cannot be my life. There has got to be more. I know God blessed me with more than just this. How about I give something else a try? I love to help people."

My mom, girlfriend at the time, and my boy, Kris, were saying the same thing,

"You love to help people. Why don't you do something in health and wellness?"

I guess it finally sunk in, and that's when I did the unthinkable. I surrendered to the process and stopped trying to force it. I left the music industry, and everybody thought I was crazy. All the while, every day, I kept thinking about that same vision of winning five Grammys, walking on the red carpet with my mom, and retiring her. You would think that since I left the music industry, I was also quitting on that vision, but that was not the case. That vision was living inside of me.

Fast forward five years in a completely different industry that was geared toward transforming people's lives through health and wellness, I received a call from corporate saying that I qualified for an award show that was a yearly event based around recognition.

Can you guess where the event was held?

It was held in the exact same place they hosted the Grammys. I won five awards that night, I walked on the red carpet with my mom, and I retired her from her job all in the same night, just like I pictured it. It also gave me the exact same feeling I felt when I originally spoke the vision. That's when it hit me. It wasn't about what it was on the surface. It was more about the feeling. I realized in that moment that the feeling was the secret.

That 15-year process was my resistance. I thought it was trying to break me when, in fact, it was actually developing me. We get tested in the process of growing through circumstances, challenges, and life experiences. The process doesn't get easier; we just get stronger, and that strength will be a blessing we can use on our journey.

God's Timing

The following story might just blow your mind, so pay close attention to the series of events.

I was flying to Hong Kong, and five minutes before we boarded, I heard the following over the intercom.

"The flight to Hong Kong is canceled. Come back tomorrow at 7:00 p.m."

It was very odd. They said it was because the workers timed out. I came back the very next day at 7:00 p.m., and they canceled the flight again. It felt like Groundhog Day when they said the exact same thing on the intercom.

"The flight to Hong Kong is canceled." All of a sudden, everyone ran to customer service, and I thought to myself, *"There is no way I'm going to wait in line while 200 angry people try to get rebooked on a different flight."*

I knew if I took another flight the next day that I would completely miss the entire first half of the event where I was scheduled to speak. I walked downstairs to ask about a new flight, and the stewardess said everything was completely sold out. I was going to throw in the towel because there was literally nothing I could do, but I asked again,

"Are you sure there are no more available flights?"

The lady said,

"Wait a minute! I literally have one more flight, but it's on a completely different airline." I said I would take it. I quickly headed over to Korean Air, and they let me know that I would stop in Seoul, South Korea and transfer, then head to Hong Kong. I kept saying to myself, *I know God is trying to tell me something.* Also, the fact that I was being rerouted to Seoul, South Korea was cool in itself because I had gone there earlier in 2018, and the name Seoul reminded me of my heart and soul.

Now my girlfriend, Blair, left from a different state at a much earlier time, and I had no clue what flight she was on. My assistant told me that her assistant *accidentally* booked her flight to Hong Kong on a different day than she was originally supposed to leave, but they just rolled with it.

Fifteen hours later, I arrived in Seoul, South Korea, and as I was walking to my gate, I looked to my left. I literally thought I was seeing things because Blair was sitting in a café. I looked again, and the first thing I said to myself was

"But of course!" I yelled out Blair's name, and when she looked up, it was as if she was seeing things. She ran to meet me and asked,

"What are you doing here? I thought you were in Hong Kong." I said, "I thought you were in Hong Kong because you left way before I did."

I thought it was really cool because I flew down on Korean Air, and she flew down on Delta. That's when we both realized that our connecting flight was the exact same flight. Now, if that is not divine timing, I don't know what is. I knew God was trying to tell me something, but I didn't know it was to connect me with my soulmate in Seoul, South Korea and be on the exact same flight, something that we did not originally plan.

The process was so trusted that it caused two canceled flights, a re-booking, a change in airlines, one accidental booking date, two different airlines, and all to unknowingly meet up during a layover in a different country... and all of this to be on the exact same flight with Blair.

I'm sure that it's not surprising to know that Blair is now my wife. I knew she was the one from our very first date. She was the very first woman I had ever been with where when I looked at her, I could see my future. It was like a portal opened up. That night is when I actually told her how I felt. I trusted the process that was going on inside of me. My intuition was so strong and I had faith to see it through.

To add even more to the story, as we were connecting more and more, I just so happened to find my 3-year-old journal. In it was sixty-two attributes that I wanted in a soulmate. To be honest, I didn't think that person existed but when I read Squire Rushnell's "When God Winks" and it talked about attracting your soulmate, I decided to write my list.

On the top of my page I wrote "Whoever has all sixty-two of these attributes will be my soulmate. We will get married and have two kids." I also wrote how I would like to feel in the relationship, and I wrote the top five places that I've never been before that I would meet this person. I circled and starred "Personal Development seminar."

Fast forward three years to when I found my journal and met Blair. I read all of the attributes and to my amazement, Blair had literally all sixty-two attributes. She treated me exactly how I wrote down, and guess where we met? Yes, at a personal development seminar! So now you see why the Honk Kong trip was so significant. Two months after I found my soulmate journal, this is what happened.

Through any process, I've learned that what I want wants me. However, I must be available to receive it. I must have a clear vision or goal.

HAVE FAITH, make a powerful choice to start where I am and press toward the mark.

HAVE FAITH, trust the process.

HAVE FAITH, grow through the process.

HAVE FAITH, be grateful along the way.

HAVE FAITH, learn the lessons and develop into the kind of person that could physically hold space for that vision.

GIVE GRATITUDE, stay calm, and flow.

This is what it means to *trust the process*.

Now, think about your life. You are currently in a process. It could be a financial process, soulmate process, moving process, divorce process, courthouse process, death in the family process, or a health and wellbeing process.

The first step is to simply be aware that you are in a process. We cannot change what we are not aware of.

The second step is to get clear on your vision for your life. You can't hit a target you don't have.

The third step is to get clear on exactly *why* you want what you want. When the *why* is greater than the *what*, the *how* doesn't matter.

The fourth step is to completely give up any attempt to force the outcome. Trust that it is all working in your favor.

EXERCISE:

Take out a clean sheet of paper and write down three times in your life when you were growing through a process and eventually got the result that you wanted. Then write down all the lessons you learned through that process. This is a clear formula for any opportunity of growth that comes your way. The intention is to train your mind to see the good in every situation. A mind that knows the sun is always out even when it's storming, will always be connected to the light. Remember to **trust the process.** Inside of trust lies your faith. Inside of faith lies access to co-creation, and when co-creation is present, the miraculous in life occurs. Like my mom always says,

"Do your part and God will handle the rest."

I'm a Walking Prayer

|Garrain Jones

It's been eight years since I've written a song, rhyme
scheme, or anything of that nature,
but right now my heart just spilled out all over the paper.

This is my story of truth I must share.
For it is my intention for you to compare
yourself to yourself as you stare in the mirror.
for those who seek help you will find it right there.
Blessings on blessings on blessings … I'm a walking
prayer!

All that I have I do not own
the tokens of gratitude belong to the throne
the most high in agreement to signs that have shown

I simply obey for the seeds to be sown
because before I was born the trumpets were blown

That I in His eyes the world needed Jones
but Jones was lost for selfish had grown

I felt so invisible like dead and alone
til one night I cried to the Creator's throne

Okay! Okay! Okay! I screamed and I moaned
Just show me a sign. I won't do you wrong!

I surrendered my life to the skies of unknown
and a voice came over me and said, "Son, welcome home."

It's been eight years of righting my wrongs
the lessons I've learned created new songs
I sing with my heart through lessons to bond
the message we need for us to move on
he sacrificed me the sound of the gong
woke up in a sea the impact was strong.

I'm awake! I'm awake! I'm awake! Are you there!
I'm so grateful to be alive! I just want to be clear!
You are in him, her, And you are everywhere!
So to you my agreement! Global impact I'll share
without you I'm nothing
but with you I am a walking prayer.

Thank you. Thank you. Thank you. Father,
Son, and the Holy Spirit
I know you're there.

The photo is from my old storage unit that I used to live out of during the day, sleeping on a pile of junk three feet high.

This is your life and how it begins

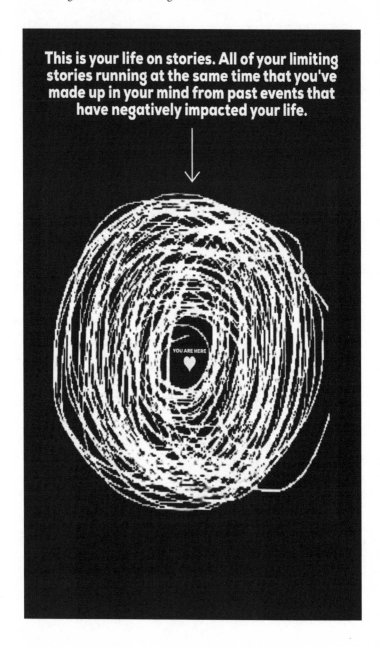

These are limiting stories

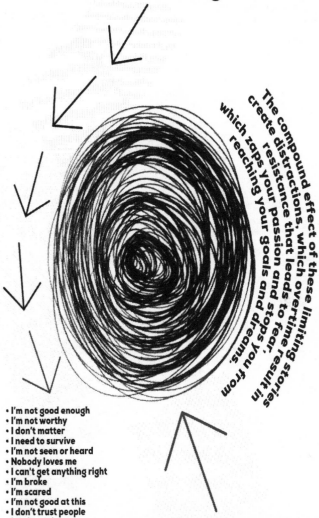

The compound effect of these limiting stories, which overtime create distractions that leads to fear, resistance in which zaps your passion and stops you from reaching your goals and dreams.

- I'm not good enough
- I'm not worthy
- I don't matter
- I need to survive
- I'm not seen or heard
- Nobody loves me
- I can't get anything right
- I'm broke
- I'm scared
- I'm not good at this
- I don't trust people
- Im always late
- My parents don't love me

Invisible wall of fear

"On the other side of your fears is the door to more."

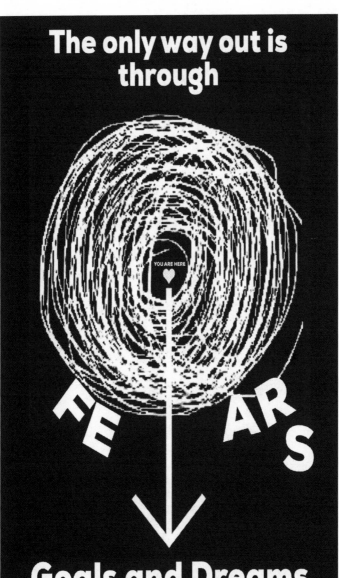

Just know that you will be tested because these limiting stories don't go away. You can't change what happened to you. However, you can change how you respond to what happens to you and what you focus on.

CHAPTER 2

The Tests of Life

*We are not going through life;
we are growing through life.*

Since I was a kid, I have always believed that there was gold at the end of the rainbow. Though I never heard any success stories of someone discovering that gold, as I grew older, the reason hit me. I never heard about many people discovering the gold because they gave up too soon. As children, we were never taught how hard it would be to find the gold because there were so many tests along the way in order to get there. Now, I can honestly say that I have discovered gold while growing through the tests of life, and I wanted to share with you everything I've learned so that you may discover your life's gold as well.

Trust the Process

"God, who do you need me to become in order to change my life?"

These were words that I yelled when I just couldn't take it anymore. The same things kept happening in my life over and over, and I couldn't figure out why. What I didn't know is that I was being tested to see if what I wanted is what I really wanted. This test is a compound of distractions that is known as resistance. This resistance morphs into fear. Even though the tests were trying to break me, I learned that whenever I passed a test, I strengthened my willpower, which allowed me to be mentally stronger to move closer towards my goals and dreams.

All my life I was taught to leave the past in the past, not realizing that it kept repeating itself. My future was literally a manifestation of my past, which was trying to teach me a lesson.

In my darkest hours, I often asked God why the same things kept happening to me in life. I couldn't seem to figure out the answer. I couldn't understand why I kept attracting the same type of girl, the same kind of jobs, and why I was distracted by the same poor choices which kept me broke, complaining, and alone. I would gain moderate success and momentum, but I couldn't sustain it. I resisted learning from the ups and downs and kept getting up, only to be knocked back down again.

There are some things you have to grow through, just like the metamorphosis of the butterfly in Chapter One, "Trust the Process."

Since elementary school, we have all been trained for the ups and downs of life. We have been trained to take risks. Life has been teaching this all along, but there is no change without awareness.

Kindergarten is typically when kids take their first leap of faith. They must let go of their mom and dad's hands and enter a new place with strangers. I remember arriving at school on the first day and letting go of my mom's hand and then running back to her. It was the scariest moment of my life at the time. But when I got into the classroom and one of the kids made a joke, I realized that school wasn't so bad after all. Slowly, the desire to go back home left. I'd survived my first leap of faith.

As you make your way through elementary school, you are taking steps and risks. There are levels you must grow through. As you progress through each grade, there are tests that are given to determine if you've understood the lessons that were taught.

There is an organized structure to the advancement of your learning. You get to the highest class in elementary, which is fifth grade, and then there is a drop. In sixth grade you are at the bottom grade in middle school and have to work your way up to eighth grade. The cycle keeps going on and in ninth grade you are at the bottom in high school and have to work your way up to twelfth grade. These are the ups and downs of the school structure. In the middle of each year, before the holidays, you take a test for the first semester. At the end of the year, you take a final exam; and if you fail the test, you must complete the grade again. If you pass the test, you move forward.

It's just like the video game Super Mario Bros. If you pass the obstacles and tests along the way and defeat the boss at the end of the round, you get to the next level; but if you don't, you have to redo the level and face the same challenges until you learn how to pass the test. This continues through every grade level and video game. Even if you look at a mountain range, you will see peaks and valleys that go up and down. When someone has taken their last breath in the hospital, there is a flatline that signifies death, and as soon as that needle jumps, notice how the ups and downs of the needle signifies life. Are you starting to notice the pattern?

This is the exact same model that the path of our life follows. The ups and downs are uniquely designed for every one of our lives. There are tests you must pass to get to the next level in life. Most people don't realize this because once they graduate from high school or college, they think that the testing and learning is complete. Actually, you will pick up right where you left off on the growth scale.

Unfortunately for me I cheated my way through school and then wondered why life after graduation was so hard. If you are thinking,

Why does the same thing keep happening to me?

It's possible that you have been failing the same tests all your life. Those tests could be failed relationships, staying at jobs you don't want, your insecurities causing you to make poor choices, giving up on your dreams, limiting your creativity or ideas, or falling into bad habits, like drugs, alcohol, resentment, blaming people, or being a victim all your life.

I feel that God has a strange and timely way of letting us know that we need to learn the lessons, whether we like it or not. If you want big things out of life, you will be tested BIG, but just remember that God designs tests the way he knows you best, and often the only way to get your attention is if the test is connected to your heart.

For example, your girlfriend suddenly breaks up with you, your dad disapproves of the guy you fell in love with, or you didn't get the raise you wanted and instead a person who is less qualified got it. You see? If it wasn't connected to your heart, it wouldn't make a difference to you. This is often why it hurts so much to be tested. It's also important to know that the test is resistance, and it will match the size of your dream. The bigger the dream, the bigger the resistance, the bigger the test. So nothing is actually happening *to* you; it is happening *for* you.

I've heard many people say, "I feel like the same thing happens to me every year around the same time." This is the test of life. If the same things keep happening to you, it is because you keep failing the same tests and wherever you are stuck in life is your school. No matter the circumstances you were born into—wealth, poverty, private education, the streets, positive environments, negative influences— you will have to learn how to navigate the terrain, learn from the failures and mistakes you make, and rise from the falls you take.

There will always be tests and lessons you must learn in life. Some tests you will pass and some you will fail. The question is, are you consistently showing up to class and being a willing student, or are you skipping school, thinking you know best, ignoring the guidance from those who came before you, and repeating the same patterns that keep you stuck?

Eventually you will have to take that test—the pride test, the ego test, the growth test. Everyone has to do their homework in order to pass the test of life. Just remember to trust the process and know that you do not have to do it alone. There will always be someone in your life who can pull out of you what you can't pull out of yourself if you learn to pay attention. When the student is ready, the teacher will show up. Just like in the video game, Zelda, there is a wise owl along the way supporting us to get through the road ahead. In life that owl shows up on our journey as a teacher, neighbor, basketball coach, or even the homeless man on the street. The question is, have you made yourself available to listen? Trust the process. It's trying to tell you something and help you grasp a lesson so you can move forward. It doesn't take preparation, just awareness and faith. **You don't have to get ready if you stay ready.**

EXERCISE:

Write down three of your biggest tests in life that you feel have power over you. Just know that whatever has power over you becomes your god. It becomes the maker of your life. They could be any of the following: women, men, money, alcohol, drugs, fatty foods, hoarding, gossip, TV, your relationship, the job you always complain about. Now is your opportunity to do something different. Change your mindset, change your life. It's what we do about it and how we can look at the situation from a different perspective that creates the result. When you discover the lesson, welcome your tests with gratitude and say these words out loud:

> Thank you for being a great teacher. Thank you for making me better. Thank you for making me stronger. Thank you for making me wiser.

> You will be surprised at how much strength lies in the embodiment of those words. What happens to us, happens to us all mentally. We don't know what we don't know, so it is important to seek teachers, places of worship, coaches, mentors, transformation seminars, positive communities and books to ultimately develop a relationship and be closer to God, which will ground you and restore your power. This will make the difference and guide you through the tests of life.

What addresses are in your mental gps system?

GPS

"Whichever thoughts you give the most power and energy to whether it's positive or negative, shows up as the physical equivalent in your life."

Possible addresses
in your mental gps system

Gossip
Toxic relationships
Negativity
Pride
Transformation
Healthy Active Lifestyle
Fear
Comparing
Jealousy
Ego
Competition
Trying to remember a lie
Stress
Global Impact
Positive Thinking
Goals
Being unhealthy
Leadership
Asking yourself "what's wrong with me?"
Selfless Service
Joy
Questioning your greatness
Love
Hate
Attracting your soulmate
I'm ugly
Nobody likes me
Drugs
Alcohol

"I got 99 blessings and negativity ain't one"

"Energy goes where energy flows"

Do you have a PMA?

Positive Mental Attitude

That perfect person will never walk into your life until the day you realize that perfect person is you.

How you treat yourself is a direct reflection of what and who you are attracting in your life.

A positive mental attitude and self love is a must

Your soulmate is waiting for you

"The outside is the physical manifestation of what's going on inside the brain."

CHAPTER 3

The Power of Positive Thinking

*The outside is the physical manifestation of
what's going on inside the brain.*

I grew up in a very negative environment. So every time I saw people speaking positively, it was like alien talk to me, and I thought they were fake. Even though there were positive things that took place in my life when I was younger, I remember what I focused on most was everything that had to do with negativity. I didn't know any other way to be. Though deep down inside I knew there was more to life, my negative mentality completely blinded me to the possibilities that were outside of that negative lens I was looking through every day.

When I was 18 years old, my friend, Shannon Davidson, gave me a book for my birthday. The book was *The Power of Positive Thinking* by Norman Vincent Peale. To be honest, I thought it was the stupidest gift, especially because I hated reading, not to mention that in high school

I had a speech impediment and was in special needs classes. I already thought I was stupid because I learned slower than 95 percent of the students in my grade. Why would anyone give me a book?

That book sat on my shelf for months. Then one day out of frustration from always going into my shell when I heard other people use big words and passion when speaking, I picked up that book not aware of what it was about. I started reading and overenunciating my words, not knowing what the outcome would be. With my mouth wide open and sounding out every vowel, I read that entire book out loud.

It took me one focused week to read the book and by the time I was done and went back to talking normally, I noticed the most miraculous thing had happened. I had a bigger vocabulary, and my speaking impediment magically seemed to be gone. In addition, positive things were happening in my life. I had no clue it was from what I had read in the book and how I was unconsciously applying biblical principles with a positive mental attitude. I thought it was all luck and chance. I wasn't aware of what I was attracting into my life because of my new thought conditioning.

Here are a few things that took place with my new, positive outlook on life. I signed a contract with Wilhelmina Models, one of the top modeling agencies in Los Angeles. Beyoncé handpicked me from a photo to be her love interest in the Destiny's Child "Jumpin' Jumpin'" video. I booked a six-figure paying job with L'Oréal Hair for a worldwide commercial, and I barely had any hair.

I was low on money and was about to be evicted from my apartment, and while walking down the street, I just so happened to step on a wad of money that was the exact amount I needed for rent. I posted on social media that I could see myself meeting one of my favorite athletes Conor McGregor and that three people would be around. Literally eighteen days laters, I had met Conor McGregor and three people were around just like I positively visualized. It was as if I would think of something, and it would show up in physical form. I didn't know what to make of it, but clearly something out of the ordinary was happening. I called it "being in the swirl," which reminded me of what happens when you shake a snow globe and the flakes come floating down. In this case, random miracles were being attracted into my life.

When I finished reading the book, there was a massive amount of momentum flowing through me. So many amazing things were going on in my life and I had no clue where it was all coming from. I never knew that what you expose your mind to could effect the way that you think. I stopped reading because I thought all I needed to do was read or hear it once and I was good for life. My, how I was wrong. People started praising me and telling me I was the man. That's when it started to set in and I said to myself, "I'm the man. I know so many people want to be me."

Yes, you know it.

Ego had crept in, and just as fast as I started attracting all these amazing things in my life, once my attitude turned negative again, I started to lose everything because I wasn't aware. I had no clue that I had full control over what was happening.

Fast forward 21 years as I have connected the dots when I look back on my life. Every time I've had a positive mental attitude toward everything and backed that up with action, the most amazing things have taken place. And every time I had a negative mental attitude, it was taken away, as if I wasn't deserving of abundance in my life.

I was at a wellness workshop and heard a powerful leader say that you must always do everything you can to maintain a positive mental attitude because the second you let up, your old life of negativity will creep back in. I knew without a shadow of a doubt what I needed to do from that moment. I needed to continuously keep feeding my mind with everything that served a purpose in moving me toward any goal I wanted in life, while maintaining a positive mental attitude.

Our mind is like a garden, and our thoughts are the seeds we plant in the garden. Whatever we plant, will indeed grow, whether they are seeds of positivity, seeds of negativity, seeds of doubt, seeds of gratitude, or seeds of not feeling worthy. The soil of our minds is watered by the thoughts that we give the most power to. The garden must be tended, and the second we leave the garden, the weeds start creeping in. EGO! The weeds of your mind, of your past, come back to take over.

By applying positive thinking in everything you do, in every circumstance, and through every challenge, it will eventually create an overflow. This is the overflow that has poured out as physical evidence in my life and didn't just happen overnight.

Even when I was living in my car, it made me feel so good to create positive communities to see other people smile and make friends. I had a workout movement called GUMBO—Get Up and Move Your Butt Operation—and I would train and motivate people for free at Runyon Canyon in Los Angeles, California. I did this every single Saturday and had up to 95 people at one time. When I was sleeping in my storage unit, I made the best of it and created a personal development YouTube series called "The Storage." No one had any idea how bad my life was while I was continuously pumping out content on social media, and doing my best to inspire those who needed it in their lives. I never complained. I always said, "It could always be worse! Someone else who's gone through worse has made it out and made something of their life, so why not me?" I would say that every single day and keep a positive outlook even when there was no physical proof. It wasn't about what I was doing; it was the spirit from which I was doing it.

Today I earn an incredible living doing what I would do for free, which is exactly what I was doing when I was living in my car. It was as if God was checking me to see if I was serious about what I wanted. Despite my circumstances, I carried a positive mental attitude through the process and continued to bring joy to the people from the joy that was first flowing through me.

Take a look at your own life at this very moment— your love life, your money life, your family life, your work life, your creative life, and your abundant life. If it's not flowing, there is a great chance that it's not getting the most positive aspects of your mental attitude. Remember, the outside is the physical manifestation of what's going on inside the brain. It's simple: Are you being positive or negative in any of those areas that may or may not be working?

I will show you exactly what's going on with your life so you can physically see what's happening in real time. Go to your sink and get a clear glass. Pour water in that glass until it reaches the brim. The water is now at a tipping point, and as you pour in a little bit more water, what starts to happen? The water starts to spill over on the outside. Now, let's imagine that you are that glass. If your thoughts are mainly negative, that is what you are pouring in that glass. The thoughts that you give the most power to are what is overflowing into the physical evidence in your life. The negative life is experiencing the overflow of what's been flooding your insides.

Now imagine all of that being positivity. The physical evidence in your life has to match. The health of the roots is what determines the growth of the tree and the fruit it produces. So now that you can see what you are clearly creating in your life because of your thoughts, how will you choose to think from this point on? Positively or negatively? Whichever you choose, welcome to your life's creation. Energy goes where energy flows.

Imagine listening to a song over and over and over and over and over. For the next month, you'll be singing and humming the song because you can't get it out of your head. The same thing applies to your thoughts. If you keep hanging around people who are negative, watching negative TV shows, gossiping, engaging in negative self-talk, or contributing to negativity in any way, you will be guilty by association. That will become your life's song that you play over and over and over. What will happen? Your life will be a physical manifestation of that negativity. Is that how you want to live your life?

Do something about it while you can. Turn all your thoughts and actions toward whatever contributes to your dreams and goals. There's no right or wrong, only new levels of awareness. Let this experience be the one that wakes you up and alters the course of your life as well as that of the people around you who will benefit from your shining example. Be and stay positive, my friends.

EXERCISE:

For an entire week, look for the positive in everything that has to do with anything. If someone cuts you off on the road, find the one thing positive in that. If your boss at work yells at you for no reason, look for the seed of positivity inside that. If it starts thundering and you planned a huge picnic with your family, look for the positivity in that.

The more your positive inward focus flows into your outward look on life, the more the pendulum of your life will, indeed, show up positive.

WHY IS BEING HEALTHY SO IMPORTANT?

Your health affects your heart

What you do to your heart affects how you feel

How you feel affects the way you think

How you think affects the way you speak

How you speak affects your actions

Your actions affect the outcome of your life

80% nutrition
20% fitness
100% mindset

Say YES to H.A.L

"40 is the new 20 if you're healthy"

CHAPTER 4

Frankenstein Comes to Life

*To not care about your health, is to be dead
while still living.*

Growing up, "being healthy" was never a conversation topic at home. Therefore, there was no way my family could understand the concept of "being healthy" much less practice it.

There was nothing health-conscious about our diet. We grew up on Southern cuisine that was just fatty, fried, and unhealthy. Though it was the stuff clogged arteries dream of, it was damn good. However, we didn't know it wasn't good for us. We just ate what we were fed, and that was that.

I continued the same eating pattern into my 30s, and that's when the unthinkable happened. I was putting on weight and growing out of my clothes. My waistline went from a size 31 to 36, and my weight went from 150 pounds to 200 pounds. This happened within three years, and I was so embarrassed of myself that I couldn't manage to look at the scale, and I stopped looking at myself in the mirror. My skin was super dry, and my allergies were out of control. I could not stop the cycle. I surrendered to defeat and gave up on myself.

Frankenstein was Dead

I chalked it up to my age. I would say things like,

"Well, I guess this is what happens when you hit 30, so what's the use in trying."

I became extremely insecure about my appearance, and I felt even worse on the inside. I was always tired and had no energy. I would walk around sluggish all day, like a zombie. This sent me into a deep depression. Out of shame, I even reduced my postings on social media. I was always trying to find the right lighting, angle, or filter that would give a false representation of how I looked so I could post it.

The way I felt caused me to become angry and resentful. I gave out negative energy because that was how I was treating myself, and I was trying to disguise it by shaming other people to make myself feel better. Indeed, I was toxic. One day I woke up and didn't even know who I was. I didn't look or act the same. I wasn't living; I was just existing. It's hard to believe that not being healthy could cause this much damage in my life.

In November 2011, a guy named Brian who looked like a superhero took me under his wings and introduced me to his health and wellness community. It completely rocked my world. I had never seen that many positive, fit, goal-driven people in one place at one time. As much as I wanted to deny it, deep down in my soul, I knew that this was meant for me. As I continued to surround myself with this health and wellness community, things started to shift for me. Everyone was so encouraging and supportive, and I found myself wanting to do everything they were doing because they seemed to be so happy.

I learned so many things from this community that I felt were a big reason my mindset started to change, and I became open to new possibilities.

Frankenstein Started to Shake and Twitch

I was coming back to life. One of the things that stuck out was how acknowledging and caring they were to one another. Everyone wanted everyone to succeed in life, and they were so supportive of each other's goals and dreams. This was all new to me. I liked it and wanted more, so I kept going back. I was introduced to daily personal development, writing down my goals and dreams, daily affirmations, and daily meditation, and all of this inspired me to start praying every day. Day by day, I could literally feel my brain becoming more calm and peaceful.

One day I was surfing the internet for personal development, and I heard Jim Rohn say, "How you do anything is how you do everything."

That line hit me like a ton of bricks. I looked at every area of my life, and I knew they needed to change and change for good. That was the pivotal moment when I decided I was going to take my health seriously. I wanted to live a healthy active lifestyle and I was willing to do whatever it took. I jumped right in, and though it was hard, just being around like-minded people who were up to the same thing supported me tremendously. I learned that health is 80% nutrition, 20% fitness, and 100% mindset. I had been doing it wrong—I was 100% excuses, 15% fitness, 0% nutrition, 40% complaining, with an added bonus of two percent action. It's no wonder I felt like Frankenstein. My actions did not represent someone who gave themselves the best opportunity to truly live.

I jumped in and started a customized nutrition program, where I was taking supplements, eating healthy balanced meals, drinking plenty of water, and exercising three to four times a week.

Frankenstein Came to Life

This 80% nutrition was very new to me, and I quickly saw and felt a massive difference. My energy shot through the roof. Naturally, I wanted to do more because I wasn't falling asleep in the middle of the day every day. I felt like my soul was rebooting itself, and my body followed. Frankenstein came to life! Ahhhhhhhh, I got my mojo back! I got back in the gym with the excitement of a kid staring at his presents on Christmas day.

When you give your body the fuel it is supposed to have, it has the ability to work how it is supposed to work. In three and a half months I dropped 39 pounds and took my body fat from 16.4 percent down to six percent. Then I decided to put on 19 pounds of muscle. I felt like a superhero. I was on fire. It was a new me. Actually, it was the real me.

The compliments poured in from left and right. I was even getting compliments from people who didn't like me a few months prior.

What the heaven was going on?

Who was I becoming?

Everything was happening so fast. Thank God, I had a support group of like-minded individuals who were there step by step throughout the process. A positive community and accountability made everything so much easier. Who would've ever thought that working toward being the best version of myself would start the process that would open me up to the transformational change that most people on this planet seek?

As night turned to day, my world was turned upside down and inside out. Everything was changing, including my friends. Gandhi's words started to make sense,

"Be the change you wish to see in the world."

My outside world was starting to match my inside world.

This was now my community. I was a reflection of my environment, and my environment was a reflection of me. What was once met with doubt now turned into admiration as many people outwardly expressed that they wanted what I had: Energy, to be physically fit, a positive community, joy, confidence, and self-love. When you have something so good, only a greedy person would keep that to themselves. I powerfully chose to share the gift of health and wellness all over the world, impacting millions of lives directly and indirectly. Throughout this journey I can't tell you enough the level of joy it brings to my heart knowing all the transformational change that has taken place in the lives of friends, family, strangers, and even old enemies. Haters need health and wellness in their lives too.

The most powerful transformation that I am most proud of is that of my mom, Sherian Jones, aka Momma Jones. In 2011, she was very unhealthy and on the verge of losing her life. She was on more than ten different medications, extremely overweight, had several surgeries, and a colostomy bag. I was so mad because I didn't think I could do anything about it.

I want you to stop right now and think about your mom, dad, or someone really close to you who is not healthy and how precious they are to your heart. Really take time to read what I just shared about my mom. Now imagine what would be going through your mind, knowing you couldn't do anything to help that special someone in your family. Well, I got sick and tired of seeing my mom like that, so I made a commitment to not only live a healthy, active lifestyle for myself, but for my family.

Through this process, I learned that people don't do what you say. They do what they see. My mom saw me transform my life, and she wanted the same. I introduced her to the health and wellness lifestyle, and she took it on and started getting her life back as well. She stayed consistent because I was the example of consistency, and her life was a major motivator. It's amazing what happens to one's choices once they get a taste of death. It is now seven years later, and my mom has maintained the 70 pounds she lost, and she no longer has a colostomy bag, has had no more surgeries, and takes no medications. At the age of 64, she is now the happiest she has ever been.

She now rock climbs, does aqua fit, goes ziplining, and has decided to follow her dreams of becoming a fashion designer and even launching an eyewear line. Just imagine the amount of people whose lives you can transform by being a health advocate.

We are empathic beings by nature, and our hearts are at the core of it all. We can only reach a certain level of happiness if we are not healthy. By following this formula, you will see how it is all connected.

Your health affects your heart.

What you do to your heart affects how you feel.

How you feel affects the way you think.

How you think affects the way you speak.

How you speak affects your actions, and your actions affect the outcome of your life.

Recycle, rinse, repeat and share this awareness with as many people as possible. Today, I am 40 years young and in the best shape of my life. I feel electric, vibrant, joyfully spirited and like I'm in my 20's again. I truly believe that 40 is the new 20, if you're healthy.

So now you see how the better you feel, the better your life. Imagine waking up tomorrow feeling better than you've ever felt. Imagine not falling asleep every day in the middle of the day. Imagine having so much energy that you truly feel alive and full of vitality and zest. Imagine looking and feeling how you really want to look and feel. Imagine not having to overcompensate in other areas of your life to distract from the fact that your health is not a priority.

Imagine wearing the clothes you truly want to wear.

Imagine being so secure and confident that you don't have to take pictures at certain angles or with special lighting and filters, because you look good at every angle and in every lighting.

Imagine your family and friends being inspired by your personal change and wanting to join you because it's something they always wanted to do; they just needed an example. Imagine being that example.

If you are playing the imagination game and you allowed yourself to imagine all these things, you should be feeling a different sensation in your body right now. That sensation is possibility in motion. It's what is possible for your life every day. Your health is something to take very seriously. Don't wait until it's too late, like most people do. We are not cars. When the transmission dies because the engine wasn't taken care of, it can be replaced with a new one. When we die due to health-related issues that could've been prevented, we don't get a second chance.

Being healthy and taking care of your temple, mind, body, and spirit, can truly open your eyes and heart to what it means to love yourself. You can't give what you don't have; and if you give out so much to everything and everyone else but forget yourself in the process, you are giving out 100 percent from the two percent you give to yourself. You might as well walk around with a shovel all day, digging yourself an early grave. I'm not exaggerating. I cannot stress how important this subject matter is. Health is wealth, and you can offer so much more to the rest of the world when you are at your best for YOU. You want people to benefit from the overflowing of love you have first given yourself.

EXERCISE:

1. Take out a clean sheet of paper and write down your weight-loss or fitness goals. Or maybe you just want to feel better about yourself and have tons of energy. Write it down and then write a specific date that you will take action and make that happen.

2. Then write down a list of at least 10 people in your life who you would want to be on this journey with you. Ask them to join you on this journey and hold you accountable.

3. Find a community of goal-driven people who are living a healthy, active lifestyle and surround yourself with them on a continuous basis. You can find these communities either online or in person.

4. Commit to finding a wellness coach or someone who can support you with your nutrition intake. Remember, food is fuel, and it's 80% nutrition, 20% fitness, and 100% mindset.

5. I invite you to head over to my website at GarrainJones.com and download my free guide, 20 Ways to Jumpstart a Healthy Active Lifestyle. That should be enough to get you started.

What if everything that you've been looking for has been inside of you this entire time?

"The longing for more that we seek lies in the fulfillment of our hearts"

"Love begins at home, and it is not how much we do but how much love we put in that action."
Mother Theresa

"What comes from the heart goes into the heart"

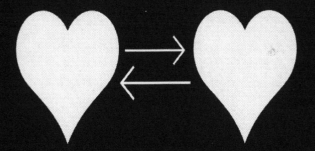

"To honor what is in your heart is to nourish your inner child which taps into your spiritual umbilical cord to heaven."

CHAPTER 5

Do What You Love

*To honor what is in your heart is to nourish
your inner child which taps into your spiritual
umbilical cord to heaven.*

The test of life began when I was a little kid. I loved pandas, colorful socks, singing, dancing, running, my mom's smoothies, my Big Momma's sweet potato pie, bow ties, fashion, roller skating, primary colors, collecting basketball and football cards, soft batches of strawberry Twizzlers, room temperature orange Gatorade, pretending I was a superhero, playing "that's my car" and "that's my house" with my brother and cousins, recess, family reunions, when the sun came out, when the sun went down, rain, sleet, snow, the sound of the wind, and getting the prize in a happy meal from McDonald's. The list goes on and on, but I think you can tell that I pretty much loved everything.

It's no wonder I was always happy and filled with what seemed like unlimited amounts of energy. I found love and gratitude in all things, but that was not modeled to me by anyone. I realized I was born happy; it was already inside me. Our natural state is joy. Just take a look at kids. They are born full of love and happiness.

As I grew older, things began to change. There were more options to experience, more opinions to hear, more rules to follow from those in authority, telling me what I needed to do, what I should do, and what I'd better do. There were more kids at school bullying me and making fun of me, more negativity from the news, and the influence of society telling me what was the most popular and widely accepted thing I should do or have in my life… and I picked up on all of it. I was drowning in a sea of negativity.

There were so many people in my life who either made fun of me or talked poorly about things I loved that, one by one, I abandoned what I loved so I could slowly but surely fit in with the norm. This caused the birth of "Prove-it Pete", a character I made up in my mind who was always trying to prove himself to others in order to seek approval and fit in.

I had no clue that abandoning the things I loved that brought me so much joy was the first stage of losing the truest essence of who I was.

If you have ever said, "I feel like something is missing," it could be because you've lost sight of the things that brought you the most joy as a child. The things you loved as a child represent your inner child, which is directly connected to your spiritual umbilical cord to heaven—I call this your source energy. If a child tapped you on your leg and said, "Mom, Mom. Dad, Dad," and you ignored them for 20 years, imagine what that relationship would be like. It would look and feel like something was missing. The soul of the child would be crushed because it hasn't been nurtured. So imagine what happens to the soul of your inner child when you ignore all the things that made you the happiest for 20 years. For example, you might be walking around and an idea hits you out of nowhere, trying to get your attention, and you ignore it for whatever reason. That was your inner child tapping on your soul, saying, "Mom, Mom or Dad, Dad." Or you might say to a friend, "I used to love dancing when I was a little kid."

And you know that you haven't danced in 10 or 15 years for whatever reason. That was your inner child tapping on your soul who wanted to come out and play. This is the part that could be missing. It is the purest essence of your soul not being paid attention to. This often creates emptiness inside of us and the feeling that something is missing.

I first learned about this concept unconsciously when I was five years young. I was at Aunt Yvette and Uncle Keith's house for our family's annual Christmas party. The adults were drinking and being loud while the kids were in the front of the room showing off their singing and dancing skills to whatever music video came on MTV. This was something new to me, and even at the age of five, I was afraid of doing new things in front of people because I didn't want to mess up. However, the thought of them cheering for me inspired me to want to put myself out there. All I really wanted was for everyone at the party to say, "Good job!" This was my shot.

I remember it as clear as day. Michael Jackson's *Moonwalker* came on. It was my turn to showcase my skills in front of my family. I started singing and doing all of Michael Jackson's moves to the best of my ability when the unthinkable happened. One by one, the adults started laughing at me, and a few of them said,

"Garrain! You can't sing!" Another said, "Garrain! You can't dance!" A few of the kids were saying the same. It didn't feel good. With a fake smile on my face, I kept going. Then I felt a knot forming in my stomach, and I was near tears.

That's when my dad started yelling. At first, I couldn't understand what he was yelling about because he was so drunk. He could hardly stand up, but then it became clear. He was actually standing up for me. He yelled these exact words.

"Aye! Don't you ever tell my son he can't do something! Garrain, if you love it and it makes you happy, then you do it! Do it no matter what. Do what you love. Don't listen to them. You do what you love and don't stop for anyone!"

It was in that moment that this feeling of overwhelming confidence overcame me. I kept singing and dancing, regardless of what anyone said. A major seed was planted that day.

As I grew older, I forgot what made me happy. I was living my life to fit the idea of how others thought I should live my life. It was like living in a jail cell that was inside another jail cell. I felt like I was far away from where I was supposed to be. No longer that happy kid who did what he loved, I put more energy into seeking other people's approval and doing what they wanted me to do and completely lost myself in the process.

Something was clearly missing. That was me, a 30-year-old grown man living in his car, still asking his mom to send him money so he could pay bills. You don't have to have lived my life to be able to relate to not being genuinely happy in your life.

Looking back, there were times I would unconsciously and spontaneously do what I loved. After further research, I can see that was when the most magical things manifested in my life. Random checks came from nowhere. Auditions were booked that I wasn't supposed to be on, and I randomly found the exact amount of money I needed for rent when my roommate spent his portion on drugs. I even met Britney Spears and danced with her at a nightclub, and she came to see me at my play the very next day.

I will never forget my dad telling me to "do what you love," and it has kept me happy, regardless of my circumstances. On a spiritual level, I had no idea what "doing what you love" meant to my soul. I just know that it kept me happy even when I was in prison.

I was 23 years old, and my life was full of pride, ego, selfishness, and greed. I ended up with a 12-year sentence in a French prison for smuggling 6.2 kilos of heroin. I knew I was being paid for doing something sketchy, but I didn't know I was smuggling drugs when I was paid to drive a car across the border.

In prison I kept asking myself,

"How did I get here? I'm so far away from where I'm supposed to be."

That narrative was like a broken record. To my knowledge, my life was over. Then one day, we were allowed to watch the movie *Shawshank Redemption*, which just happened to be based in prison, about someone who was framed for murder and was trying to prove his innocence. One line in the movie gave me the keys to my freedom. Tim Robbins said, "They can take everything they want from me, but they can't take away my mind." After hearing that line, my brain exploded with an epiphany. It was in that moment that I mentally became a free man, regardless of my circumstances. As long as I am doing what I love, then I will always be free. "Do what you love." I closed my eyes, and I said it again, "Do what you love." I knew my dad was with me. "As long as I'm doing what I love, I will always be free."

I realised I had buried the essence of my soul, aka inner child alive. From there I got back to singing, dancing, drawing, running, creating, inspiring people and bringing joy to their lives despite my circumstance. Let's just say that when freedom became part of my nature, my 12-year sentence lasted six months, and the 6.2 kg of heroin that they tested three times just happened to be fake, and they let me go. I was reading the bible, a book on positivity, and started to doing and being what I loved, and that embodied the characteristics of freedom. I felt free. To the point, I was now actually a free man. "The outside is the physical manifestation of what's going on inside the brain."

So every time you get an urge of creativity or remember something that made you so happy as a child, remember that is your inner child tapping on your soul, trying to get your attention. It is longing to be nurtured. Here lies the source of most of the unhappiness in the world.

Knowing that, will you keep ignoring and distancing yourself from the things you love, or will you begin to explore, love, nurture, and cultivate happiness back into life? If you are born with this already inside of you, then the second you leave it, you are functioning as something you are not.

I believe the essence of who we are is love; this is what we are born to be. When we do things we love, we tap into our authentic nature. We are in flow with the universe. Where love is, God is because I truly believe that God is love.

EXERCISE:

Journal or take out a clean sheet of paper and write down three things that you loved to do that brought you the most joy as a child. It could be playing in the rain, counting the stars at night, painting, dancing, or climbing a tree. Whatever sparked joy. I call these soul amplifiers. Begin to incorporate these soul amplifiers into your life at least once a week. Let that feeling of love overflow inside of you. Remember, a child needs constant reassurance of nurturing, loving, and caring, and so does your inner child, so be consistent. Activating your heart and amplifying the love inside of you is the key to elevating your energy. Use this energy to fuel your actions. Over time, you will start to notice things and people shifting around you. Continue to journal the process because you will see your life's blueprint adjust according to the love you see and authentically feel in yourself.

Love is my religion
I AM
Who are you?
I AM *love*
God is Love
Love is God
God is the universe
The universe is a reflection of what's inside of me
The God out there is the exhale I breathe
We are God
God is we
I AM *you*
I AM *me*
I AM *God*
God is she
God is **I AM**
I AM *is creation*
God, is that you?
What's your translation?
God is me
I AM *that* **I AM***!*
God is free
Just follow the plan
I and my father are one, but He is greater than I.
I chose to follow the son, now my wings are
ready to fly.
I AM. I AM. I AM.

| Garrain Jones

"What's inside of us flows the same spirit that's inside of what makes the flowers grow.
Only, the fruit we produce is peace, love, joy, and wealth in abundance.
So why put off the opportunity to continuously grow?"

"The essence of life is growth"
Jim Rohn

"Your future is being held hostage by the resistance of what you're holding onto."

"Create space to make room for your blessings"
Touré (PT) Roberts

CHAPTER 6

Upgrade Season

"Create space to make room for
your blessings."

Touré (PT) Roberts

Have you ever been so stressed and distracted by life that your thoughts start piling up on one another? Have you noticed that when you can't think straight or focus, there just so happens to be a lot going on in your life that you can't seem to manage?

Have you felt like you were stuck in mental quicksand and just couldn't seem to figure out how to get out?

Do you not find it odd that when you feel like this, it just so happens to be the time when you have the most arguments, car wrecks, cracked screens, run out of storage space on your phone, have a dirty living space, drop things, lose things, end relationships, get fired, and the list goes on. This is because the outside is the physical manifestation of what's going on inside the brain.

When we lack clarity and are not focused, we fall victim to mental hoarding, which manifests into the physical.

If you don't let go and release that which doesn't serve you, clutter will start to collect, and collect, and collect. Before you know it, you've accumulated a lot—a lot of junk, a lot of resentment, a lot of hate, a lot of whatever you've collected and accumulated over time.

You could be enjoying all the beautifulness that was destined to be in your life, but because you haven't let go of a lifetime's accumulation of feelings and emotions, there isn't any room for what you want. Hanging on to the old is an expression that you aren't deserving of an abundant life.

Think about those times when good things came into your life. Where did they come from? It's like all these things and all these people just came out of nowhere. But things don't just happen. Your life is responding to you. Before it happened, you let go of something. You surrendered. You made room for something or someone new to come into your life. You may not have been aware of it, but you were the cause of it all.

After you release the old, you're literally closer to your authentic nature. That's where you want to be; it's who you were born to be. Think about babies. You've never seen a hateful baby. You've never seen an insecure baby. Hate and insecurities are the by-products of domestication. These are things that clog the mind and create mental clutter. This is a learned behavior. People don't do what you say. They do what they see, and they respond to how they feel.

Look back at the last five to ten years of your life. Are you still wearing the same clothes? Do you show up the same way, get mad at the same things, have the same attitude, and say the same things you always have? Are the results in your life still the same? If so, it is time for a change. I call this upgrade season.

If you were to ask all the people in your life today if they have a rotary phone or a pager as their main source of communication, do you think they would say "yes" or "no"? They would say "no" because times have changed, and the majority of society has grown with the times, which includes technology.

Now think of yourself as a phone. I'm aware that there are many different kinds of smartphones, but for the sake of simplicity, I'm going to speak about the iPhone. If you were to ask all the people in your life who have an iPhone what model they have, what would the majority say?

Would they have the iPhone three as their main source of communication? Nope! What about the iPhone four? Okay, maybe a few people still do. What about an iPhone five? Maybe 10 people? How about an iPhone six? Of all the people you know, probably more than 70 percent who own an iPhone have the iPhone seven. And now what about the iPhone 11? Is it the majority of people in your life? Why is this so? It's because technology evolves, and we let go of the old processes because they are used and outdated. When we let go of the old, we make space for the new.

Think about all the times you've had a notification for an update on your phone. Did you click *not now* or update your phone right away? The reason they create updates is because the phone is evolving with the times. Have you ever noticed what happens after a while when you don't update your phone? Your phone slows down. Could it be possible that when you continuously skip upgrades, after a while your phone breaks down, and you just so magically happen to drop your phone or the screen gets cracked? Could that be a sign from the universe that it's time to upgrade?

So hey, what about *your* upgrade? When you're noncompliant with the human upgrade, you don't lose technology. You start to lose in your life. You start losing people and opportunities. You start missing out on so many different things because you are showing up in the exact same way you always have. That's why Apple doesn't keep releasing the same iPhone with the same software. It's always an upgrade with new features.

When you become predictable and have no stimulation in your life, people around you get bored. You get bored with yourself. I think in this moment, the change your mindset, change your life philosophy could support you in a major way. So hey, why not get a haircut, get a boyfriend, get a girlfriend, get a gym membership, read a book if you usually watch TV, switch that attitude around, start taking the stairs, or take a different route to work? Just do something to add some stimulation to your life.

Upgrade season was born out of realizing that whenever you feel like you're stuck and things aren't moving or are dying around you, it's almost 100 percent directly correlated with the growth that you are not having within yourself.

This is the season when you choose what you get to let go of. The place where you feel stuck, that is your school. There's something in your life that you are just holding on to, as if "I want to hold on to the way it used to be." When iPhones come out with face recognition, nobody says let's go back to the iPhone two! People want newer and better— they want the stimulation that comes from improvement, change, and evolution.

By holding on to a bad attitude, grudges, resentments, shame, ideas, and creativity, you spiritually block yourself. We weren't created to be keepers. That's why you might feel overwhelmed at times. The weight of the world you are carrying on your shoulders is the weight of the things you keep inside that are not serving you. Like clogging up a drain when the stopper is in the way, you don't realize that's how much you are clogging up your life and leaving no room for new things to come in.

The same strength that it takes to hold on to what is not serving you is the same amount of power that's needed to elevate and sustain you at the next level. All I am asking is that you open your hands and see that you could have your desired wish if you let go of things that you're hanging on to. Like a closed hand that is opening, there is a fistful of fresh perspective.

Think about your relationships. Think about all the different things that haven't been stimulated. When was the last time you upgraded your leadership skills? When did you last upgrade your emotions and attitude? How long has it been since you upgraded your wardrobe and appearance? Are you giving everyone around you iPhone

one quality and wondering why they're not interested or stimulated when they're around you?

I invite you to stop using the same old features with the same old phone. What's the point in doing the same things you've done for the last five years if it's not working in your favor? It's time to release, add new features, and upgrade. My dad once said, "If you always do what you've always done, then you'll always get what you've always got."

My relationship with my daughter was in desperate need of an upgrade. In reality, I didn't have a relationship with her for 15 years, yet I kept trying to do the exact same thing with the same mindset. I had personal development books all over my living room about everything but parenting or understanding teens.

I started taking relationship courses and reading books about teens. I educated myself about fatherhood. It was all an upgrade. I knew I had to do something I had never done before. I asked my daughter out on a date. I learned a lot. She wanted to be heard, acknowledged, seen, and loved. She wanted me to listen. I never, ever came from that space with a woman. I just kept trying to do the same thing the same way, no upgrades whatsoever. It was an upgrade in my attitude. The new features were listening, acknowledging her, being consistent, making her feel like a priority, and making her and her mom feel safe. It's very new to me, so I've made quite a few mistakes in this process, like the mistakes that come with a new phone or learning a new language. I've got a long way to go, but I'm grateful that we've gained so much ground as a family.

Change brings growth. If you're not growing, you're dying. Everything that you create is what you're living right now. Does it happen overnight? No, it happens over time.

Whether little by little or all at once, you can't make room for your new upgrade until you release and let go of the old that you've been accumulating for years. What doesn't serve you anymore? Have you been carrying around jealousy, resentment, or anger? Release it so you can make room for new positive feelings and emotions.

A story about my friend, PJ, describes how this works. Prepare to be amazed.

Recently, I was in Arizona and visited a friend of mine, PJ. When I got there, he told me that his daughter, Ava, was suffering from nightmares and extreme temper tantrums that they didn't know were directly affected by the spiritual warfare in their house.

I spent the night at their house and heard Ava screaming throughout the night. It sounded like she was screaming for her life. I told PJ that what I heard was not a normal scream. I couldn't make sense of it, which piqued my curiosity. I was moved to start looking around. I hadn't seen the house in a long time. I started by looking in Ava's room. I looked in the garage. I looked at the dishes. I looked everywhere, and I realized that the entire house was cluttered. I asked PJ, "Do you mind if I share something with you?" He said I could. I asked, "When was the last time you deep cleaned your house?" He looked at me straight faced and said, "We've actually never done that." Then he said, "This house was formerly my mother's.

When I bought it, years of unwanted memories filled the garage and storage space to the brim."

Immediately, I replied, "Man, you've been here for at least ten years? If you've never deep cleaned your house, there could potentially be negative energy upon negative energy that has piled up here, and you're living right on top of it. I think that because children are more sensitive to energy than adults, your daughter is absorbing all of it."

It was time for an upgrade. I volunteered to help him clear the place. He and his wife, Jessica, were fine with it, so I started throwing things away that they didn't need. Because I'd grown up watching my mom collect things, I was aware of the negative energy drain that can happen when you don't create a clean flowing space. It was time for a release. When you let go of things, you make room for your blessings.

I supported PJ and Jessica in deep cleaning the house. Even baby Ava helped. We threw out some really old stuff. They got rid of an old TV that they didn't want and threw away old furniture, saying they wanted to replace it with something new. Jessica's mom had no idea what we were doing, but while we were cleaning and throwing things out, she called saying she was at a furniture store. She invited us to join her and look at some new furniture. I knew this was not a coincidence. It was all part of a specific design as we had just created this space. After looking around the store, they got one item—a new couch. And it just so happened that it was the only couch that came with a free LCD flat screen TV. It was as if their life was course correcting itself. They were able to bless someone else with that new TV and were blessed with a bigger TV from Jessica's grandfather, who passed away before I came to visit. They started developing a better understanding of decluttering, and when they cleaned out one side of the garage, they received grandfather's gracious blessing of a new car.

If that wasn't amazing enough, what happened next was clearly confirmation from above. I decided to stay with PJ a couple of extra days and changed my flight so I could support them even more. When we were done, they were clear, and Ava was sleeping better. The tantrums stopped, and they could breathe better.

I left town, and about a week later I got a FaceTime call from PJ, who looked startled. I asked what was wrong, and he said he just found a scorpion in his bedroom. I asked how that happened, and he said they were getting lazy, looked at the dusty ceiling fan and said, "Ahhh … we'll clean it tomorrow." Then one night when they were sound asleep, they both woke suddenly to what sounded like two metal pipes clanging against each other. Jessica asked PJ, "What was that sound?" PJ responded, "Hold up…" He didn't know what was going on. He sat up in the bed and felt something drop onto the sheets. He got up to turn on the light, and Jessica climbed out of the bed, and they discovered a gigantic scorpion scurrying on top of the covers. Realizing it had fallen from the ceiling fan, PJ said, "I knew God was saying we are not promised tomorrow. You are going to take care of this right now." So they did and cleaned the other three fans as well just to be safe. They cleaned the spare room, and they also cleaned the other side of their two-car garage. Later that same day, Jessica found out she was pregnant, and guess who they needed the newly cleaned room for? The baby! This was so profound because as they made room and created the space, they simultaneously made room for a new blessing in their lives.

Jump forward 18 months and they have two beautiful, healthy kids. They've completely remodeled their home and are living life on their own terms. It is the most beautiful thing to watch that kind of transformation happen.

If you feel that stale energy of sameness all over you, it's time to grow. If you start hearing people around you say, "I'm bored. I'm stuck. I'm tired or it's not fun anymore," look at your relationships. It is time to grow.

If you're not hyped up and on fire for life, I promise it's because you're not being stimulated. When you look at any area of your life that's not working, there's a lack of stimulation. Energy goes where energy flows. When your own dreams feel your energy, things will start working in your favor.

When you go through the process of releasing and letting go, you create space for the new you, new and improved features, thoughts, opportunities, and relationships. Upgrade yourself and you will have the strength that is needed for the next level of your life. It's all part of the process. When you're continuously evolving, you get to be a generator that creates potential power.

EXERCISE:

In this exercise you want to be honest with yourself about how you feel each of these areas is working in your life.

You will know what's working and what's not. It's either effective, or it's ineffective. Then on a scale of one to ten, rate yourself on your effectiveness. For the next 21 days, give focused attention to how you will upgrade and get one percent better in each of these categories.

1. Fun and Adventure
2. Health and Nutrition
3. Environment and Culture
4. Contribution
5. Personal and Spiritual Development
6. Business
7. Financial
8. Friends, Family, and Relationships

When this becomes part of your daily practice, you will start to notice power building up inside of you. This is no different than upgrading the features on your cell phone, which keeps you updated with the latest technology.

'Tis the season for upgrading. Here we grow!

Surrender

| Garrain Jones

The God I breathe is the God I see.
How beautiful it is, God's love for me.
I'm surrendering pain, down on my knees
Through resentment and shame, the pity I leave.
We break the chains, through eyes that believe.
If you are inspired, there's more to achieve.
There will be challenges, but that is the fee.
Let go and let God to uproot the tree.
It's upgrade season. There's much more to see.
This feature of love, a new update in me.
So invest in your happiness. This is the key.
For this truth from above, it will set you free.

"There is no right or wrong, only new levels of awareness.

Always trying to be right only serves the ego.

Another option could be to choose love."

"Darkness cannot drive out darkness; only light can do that. Hate cannot drive out hate; only love can do that."

Martin Luther King Jr.

"Resentment is prison"

"Apologies will set you free. Forgiveness will complete the cycle."

"If you put boundaries on love then your blessings will put boundaries on you"

"The world is dressed in black and white and love is the color"

CHAPTER 7

Love No Matter What

True love has no boundaries.

There were a series of emotional events that took place five years ago that completely altered the course of my life. As I've mentioned several times throughout this book, you cannot change what you're not aware of; and at that time I wasn't aware of how much resentment I carried in my heart or that I wasn't willing to forgive others. If someone hurt me, I would hold on to that grudge and somehow find a way to make them pay for it. If I ever hurt someone or made them feel bad in any way, I would either say, "Oh, well," and carry on with my life, or I would offer a fake apology in an attempt to create the outcome I wanted. I had no clue what this was doing to my life on a physical or spiritual level.

In my early 30s, I found myself unconsciously carrying around so much pain and resentment toward others, which was like drinking poison and hoping the other person died. I kept asking myself,

"Why does my life keep getting worse?"

Clearly, my life was responding to me and the way I was behaving.

However, this all came to a screeching halt the day I reached out to a childhood classmate who I bullied when we were seven years old. I didn't know any better when I was a kid, but I distinctly remember being on the bus and pulling her hoodie over her face and hitting her in the head with my big yellow backpack. We all laughed at her expense. In the last few years, I've seen her page on social media, and it always brought back memories of that day on the bus. I decided to reach out to her so I could apologize.

This was my exact message:

Wow! It has been forever! I hope all is well with you and your family. I know you don't remember this, but I wanted to apologize for bullying you in the second grade. Kids do the stupidest things.

She read it and didn't respond, so I decided to write a long post on my public Facebook page, literally saying the same thing. Within five minutes after it was posted, she messaged me this:

1. Could you not put the post out on FB for everyone to see? It makes me feel bad.

2. Why did you do that to me?

3. Why do you think that was done to me? I have two little boys, and it is hard to teach them about being bullied and bullying. I remember that time

and others and wonder what it was about me that warranted that treatment?

I was at a loss for words because I could not believe that people hold on to the way other people make them feel for that long. I apologized in an attempt to create space and make room for new possibilities. I could tell that she was still triggered and hurting. We continued to talk about it, which provided both of us clarity. All I wanted to do was shower her with so much love and compassion. After that conversation, I felt lighter. I now understood why there is so much pain in the world. Holding on to resentment and not being able to apologize or forgive completely stops the flow of love.

This inspired me to write a list of all the people I'd done anything negative to in actions or in thoughts. The list included the names of 250 people from kindergarten all the way up to the present moment. I also added the names of people who had hurt me, with the intention of apologizing to them for my part in the resentment that I held toward them, without any expectations as to how they would respond. I knew this was my opportunity to break the chains of my past. The hot air balloon cannot leave the ground unless you release the weight.

I apologized to each person, and after each one I felt lighter and lighter. As I was having these clearing conversations, some people would respond. Some people wouldn't, some people were still angry, and some people even apologized to me for their part. But it wasn't about their response. It was more about the process of healing myself, so I kept going. The muscle to forgive and apologize became mastery for me, which led to one of the most powerful examples that completely confirmed the title of this chapter, "Love no matter what."

Another guy and I were in the same business. We were making the same amount of income and had a very similar business model. I was an athlete, and so was he. When we were around each other, you could just feel that unhealthy competitive nature. I didn't like him, and he didn't like me, and everyone knew it. There came a time in both of our businesses when it seemed like something beyond us was keeping us in the same spot. One day I got tired of living with that internal resentment. I looked at myself in the mirror and said, "Being a friend to him has nothing to do with him being a friend to me, so I'm just going to choose to love no matter what." From that moment on, I wasn't going to let anyone else's state change who I was as a person. I made a powerful choice to be a loving nature to everyone around me, including that guy. Within the depths of my soul, I felt this strong heat vibration leap out of my chest, and I felt even lighter. Something was different. Everything started to change around me and quickly.

My spiritual guide, Monika, told me that I released hate from my heart. Within three months, my business had tripled and so did many other areas of my life. It was like holding a volleyball underwater and then releasing your hand to allow the ball to shoot up to the surface where it is supposed to be. Imagine what it's like when a dam is built to stop the flow of water. Well, I had a spiritual dam in my life called resentment; and as soon as I released it, miracles started to flow in. My business partner eventually released his resentment toward me and the same thing took place in his life and business, as well.

Then there was that time my face looked exactly like Thanos from the Avengers. I was in tears. The pain was pulsating and to make matters even worse, my jaw was double swollen. I went to see the dentist, who looked at my swollen jaw and said that he didn't have the proper tools to do the work on my teeth that needed to be done. I was told that I would need to see a specialist.

A full day of excruciating pain went by and when I saw the specialist, he said that the tooth in question needed a root-canal. None of this made sense to me because there was already a root-canal from 15 years prior in that same spot, so why would I need to get another one. The specialist said, "Whoever originally did your root canal didn't get it at the root, so you are experiencing the build-up of fifteen years worth of infection that is just now coming to the surface. In terms of dentistry your infection is the size of two football fields."

I could not believe what I had just heard and to add more drama to the story, they had to use twice as much equipment, it was twice as much work, and twice as painful. They cut half the lower right side of my jaw open and I had to pay twice as much money. All because it was never taken care of at the root to begin with.

I know this story sounds crazy but what's even crazier is the fact that I had a shift in perspective on life through this process. Picture me outstretched on a dentist chair full of anesthesia, clamping down on a six inch piece of metal with gauze and rubber keeping my mouth open. This is when I changed my mindset and my whole life changed in that very moment. I realized why I had so many unhealthy relationships in my life. They were all unhealthy at the foundation of the relationship. Just like my gums built up 15 years of infections, because the dentist never cleared out the cavity from the root, only for the outside to expose what was going on inside. The same goes for the failed relationships in my life. Whether someone hurt me, or I hurt them. Whether I held resentment or never forgave. All of that was like a cavity that was never taken care of. So it only made sense why I had unhealthy root canal like relationships.

What's beautiful is with this awareness I chose to do something about it. Just like someone could go to the dentist to get an x ray to see the root of the problem and then put together a plan to correct the problem. Do the deep work to get rid of the cavity and get a root canal. Then keep daily rituals to maintain a healthy foundation with a follow-up plan to connect and monitor the progress.

This is the exact formula that I followed to rebuild many of the relationships that I was longing for in my life. I took full responsibility for my part and x ray'd the relationships. I needed to see what was the root cause of the relationship not being healthy. To be honest, it wasn't about the other person. It was more about what part did I play in that relationship being unhealthy. I held so much resentment towards so many people and if someone ever hurt me, I never forgave them. "You've got to get all of the puzzle pieces out of the box first before you can put them together."

The destruction of my life was starting to become even more clear. This was the deep work. Once I located the cavity-like problems, I did just that. I went to work. I forgave myself for being so hard on myself or for being resentful at any point. Then I forgave other people or called and asked them for forgiveness for whatever I did. How they responded was not my responsibility because I was in full ownership for my part. This cleared the space for me to create a new possibility with them for that relationship. This was like putting a healthy crown on my tooth. Then from there, I chose to focus on the possibilities and continuously revisit it, which would turn in to a reality. This was like having regular visits at the dentist to monitor the progress.

After having so many different opportunities to exercise the muscle of apologizing and forgiveness, it gave me the strength to forgive in an area I never thought I would. I powerfully forgave the two men who murdered my father. For so many years, I wished death upon them and negative things to happen to their families. All that resentment was living inside of me like a parasite, and it was causing me to unconsciously hurt myself and those around me. I finally decided to release it and love no matter what. I powerfully chose to wish nothing but blessings for them and their families.

I told this same story on stage in front of a crowd of 2,000 people, and when I was done a man walked up to me and asked if he could speak to me. I motioned for him to come and when he walked over, he immediately said, "I want to apologize on behalf of those two men who murdered your father." I was trying to figure out the significance of this conversation.

Then he said, "Fifteen years ago I got busted for attempted murder and I just got out of prison today. I was going to kill the man who snitched on me, but after hearing your story I've changed my mind and I want to better my life." He then said, "and that's why I'm apologizing on behalf of those two men."

In that very moment, I felt this movement of energy leap out of my chest. I felt lighter and I just started crying because I never thought I would get closure from this particular area of my life. I never would've ever thought that letting go of resentment and allowing myself to forgive would equate to that sense of peace and freedom that I had been searching for since I was twelve years old.

I invite you to think about areas in your life where you haven't chosen to forgive someone or where you have been holding on to resentment for whatever reason and making people pay the price repeatedly. You are only hurting yourself if you are not coming from a loving place. If love has a condition or something needs to happen in order for you to give your love, that is not love. True love has no boundaries or conditions. Either you love, or you don't.

We reflect out how we treat ourselves within. This leads me to the most important person you will ever apologize to and forgive. That person is you. When was the last time you actually forgave yourself for how hard you have been on yourself? No one is harder on us than we are on ourselves. When was the last time you treated yourself with kindness, care, love and affection? If you took more than half a second to think about that question, then there is a good chance that you've been left out of the love equation. Remember that our lives are a manifestation of exactly how we treat ourselves. We get to create the space to make room to love ourselves no matter what. We can't give what we don't have, and you deserve to be happy.

The thing is, the only way to truly be happy is by using your heart. It's a very powerful muscle and just like any other muscle, if you don't use it it will grow weak. Strengthening the heart must be a primary focus and when given the proper exercise and nourishment, it will produce the greatest results.

Think about when you are in the gym working out. If you want to be stronger, it takes working out your muscles on a consistent basis. If you want bigger muscles, you must add heavier weight to increase the resistance. Your strength and muscles grow according to the resistance you put them through. If you are just starting out, your muscles will be really sore.

This is the exact same process for strengthening the heart. The more you intentionally exercise the muscle of your heart and choose to love no matter what from moment to moment, you will be stronger, more creative, more intuitive, more youthful, healthier, more available for loving more deeply and more available to be deeply loved. Below are a few exercises specifically for strengthening your heart. Be prepared to go where you've never gone before.

EXERCISE:

1. Write down 5 things you are powerfully choosing to forgive yourself for. Then, go to a mirror and look at yourself and say them out loud.

   You can start your sentences like this.

   I forgive myself for:
   1.
   2.
   3.
   4.
   5.

2. Write down 5 people you are powerfully choosing to forgive for whatever they did.

   I forgive you (Name):
   1.
   2.
   3.
   4.
   5.

   I forgive you for:
   1.
   2.
   3.
   4.
   5.

The possibility I would like to create for this relationship is:
1.
2.
3.
4.
5.

3. Write down 5 people you are powerfully choosing to let go of resentment towards.
   1.
   2.
   3.
   4.
   5.

Take this powerful opportunity to be in ownership and clear yourself. Reach out to them and let them know that you are in the process of transforming your life and that you want to apologize for the resentment that you've held towards them whether it was your fault or theirs. Take full responsibility for your part without any expectation of how they should respond. That is the work they get to do. From there, let them know the possibilities you would like to create in the relationship moving forward.

Here is an example of a call I made to a family member where there was no relationship. I must add that they didn't have the most positive response. However, because I wasn't focused on their response, that energy didn't bring me down. I was lifted by the possibility I created.

"Hey (Name) I'm in the process of transforming my life and I wanted to apologize to you for the resentment that I have held against you for (whatever took place). I've chosen to resent you instead of accepting the fact that you were doing the best you could with what you knew and I'm sorry. I let go of all resentment and I'm creating the possibility for us to have a fun, loving and free-flowing relationship where we are both learning from each other and nothing is in the way. "

This creates a clearing and has you pulling from the future instead of recreating more of your unwanted past. The only way to pull from the future is to create it and focus on it.

Write down 5 possibilities you would like to powerfully create for your life.

The possibilitiy I'm creating for my life is:

1.

2.

3.

4.

5.

Once you have continuously implemented these exercises, you will notice a shift in your energy and these exercises will cause your heart to grow stronger. These are the same workouts that gave my heart the strength to be able to apologize to 250 people, to forgive and apologize to the person who molested me when I was a kid, to apologize to the first girl who broke my heart and rejected me when I was in middle school, to apologize to my mom for how ungrateful I was as a kid when she was only doing her best, to forgive the two men who murdered my dad when I was 12, to apologize to my daughter for not being present and to rebuild that relationship, to forgive myself and start deeply loving myself, only to attract my soulmate who I deeply love because there is now room for her and most of all to love no matter what.

Like I said, the heart is a muscle and the more you develop the muscle to love no matter what, the more your life will reveal itself in a way that seems only to be lived in dreams. This is your choice from moment to moment, so who will you create that space for? Who will you love no matter what?

What is your purpose?

What if our purpose was grow to our maximum potential and live out all that God has called us to be?

I recognize this with nature, so why not us?

What if our mission in life was to get back to how we started?

Remember

CHAPTER 8

The Rhythm of Nature

When we truly understand the mastery of giving and receiving and how it connects us to everything that evolves, only then will we experience our authentic self walking in divine nature. That is God's tempo.

In 2013 I was hanging out with a group of leaders every day at a wellness bar. A lot of them were successful, and I couldn't understand why. I was trying to build a business just as they were, but nothing I was doing was working. I guess I couldn't see how other people saw me. I had a huge ego back then. I felt entitled. I spoke down to people. I was jealous and talked about people behind their backs whenever they would do better than me in the business. Even when I offered to help when they were looking for volunteers, I always asked myself, "What's in it for me?" When I was frustrated, I always brought up the times I helped and never got anything in return.

I worked just as hard, if not harder, than everyone else around me, but for some reason, most of them were doing better than me. I was clearly missing something. Then one day I asked the owner of the wellness bar how I could build a successful business. He said, "Here's what you can do. Always be the first person to raise your hand when it comes to contribution." I looked at him like he was crazy because all I thought about was how much are you going to pay me for helping out? It didn't make sense, but he and his wife were successful and respected among their peers, so I figured his advice was good for something. I cluelessly started volunteering around the wellness bar. I swept and mopped the floor, took out the trash, made smoothies for other people and did it all with a bad attitude. All I did was take, take, take.

On the verge of quitting, I was on a 30-minute leadership call with a top business leader and completely ignored the first 29 minutes. Then he said something that completely blew my mind. "If your business isn't working and you want to grow it, you need to find the right kind of people. And in order to find the right kind of people, *you must become the person you want to attract*."

My jaw hit the floor because it was the first time in my life that I actually cared to look at how I was showing up. "You must become the person you want to attract" did it for me. I looked at myself in the mirror and said, "The way I've been showing up, I wouldn't want to be on my own team." Everything shifted from there. I realized I had been a taker my whole life. I always wanted people to do things for me, but I never did the same in return unless I had an ulterior motive. Indeed, I was selfish.

One night while on YouTube, I heard John C. Maxwell say, "Successful people are willing to do the things that unsuccessful people won't do." I also heard the late Jim Rohn say, "Success leaves clues," and again, my jaw hit the floor. My perspective shifted. It was like I was seeing life through a different pair of lenses. I changed my mindest and started paying close attention to all the successful people around me and what they did, how they did it, how they acted, treated people, and spoke. I noticed they spoke highly of people, even when they weren't around, and uplifted others. One thing that really stuck out was how they constantly contributed without ever being asked to contribute. They also never asked for anything in return. It was as if it was part of their nature. I even saw the owner of the wellness bar ask for permission to go behind his own bar to get some water.

This way of being was new to me, and I decided to jump all the way in with this renewed mindset. I committed to an attitude of gratitude. I became a cheerful giver, offering selfless service everywhere I went. My goal was to leave anywhere and everywhere better than I found it. I discovered that "Gratitude is the glue that holds life together."

I loved bringing joy to other people's lives. Even if the job was difficult, I found a way to keep giving. Not once did I think about my business and what was in it for me. Then one day when I least expected it, an overflow of people started following me on social media. People wanted to work out with me, and they asked about my business and how they could be involved.

I had become the person I wanted to attract. My business grew in leaps and bounds, and I've created other businesses with the same servant leadership philosophy, doing ten times more than what's expected, and powerful results continue to transpire.

We weren't created to be keepers. We were created to be givers. Have you ever wondered why we have holes all over our bodies? Those holes were designed to give sweat, hair, sight, words, tears, urine, waste, ideas, creativity, etc. We were literally designed to give, and when we do, we may receive in its own timing.

Giving and Receiving is the Flow of Life

Have you ever noticed how leaves on trees and plants subtly sway back and forth or how the ocean waves sway back and forth? Even as you and I are breathing right now, the air in our lungs goes in and out, back and forth, giving and receiving. The notion of giving and receiving is part of our nature and signifies life. Everything is connected.

When you give from a selfless serving heart and allow yourself to humbly receive without expectations, you open the passage for the divine to take its course. The way many of us where domesticated by fear as children caused us to unconsciously create these blockages. We have money blockages, worthiness blockages, health blockages, faith blockages, goals and dreams blockages, and so many other blockages that stop flow from happening.

We were designed to flow, that is our nature. Answering our calling and following our dreams is in our nature.

What is your dream? That dream that's inside of you and needs to come out. Again, we were not created to be keepers. We can't even hold our breath. The more we try, the more uncomfortable it gets. If we hold our breath long enough, eventually we will die. The same thing happens if we try to hold on to our dreams, goals, creativity, ideas, resentment, forgiveness, apologies, love, gifts, etc. Something inside will die, and eventually we will manifest things that resemble death. With this awareness, we can clearly see the areas that display the act of selflessly giving and receiving. We can also see all the areas in our lives that may feel stuck and broken, and it is directly connected to the breakdown in giving and receiving.

You might say to yourself "For some reason, I can't find love" or "I can't seem to get my money right," not realizing that it's all connected. Imagine being a child and your mom or dad never taught you the values of life, never told you they believed in you or said you could accomplish anything in life. They showed you that they were always too busy to invest time in you. The child then says, "Nobody loves me. I'm not worthy of love," and grows up not feeling worthy.

Asking someone to give when they have unconsciously been blocked their entire life causes fear. This could be a major reason why most people are takers. On the flipside, there are people who give and give and wonder why they are always tired or why nothing flows in their direction. It's because the flow of nature is created by giving and receiving, not just giving or just receiving. It's the duality that counts.

I was once asked, "Garrain, what is the next level for you? You are already doing everything you love. Your life is flowing, but I want to know what is next."

I said I wanted to amplify my results in life, and I was figuring out ways to work harder. My spiritual advisor said, "Maybe it's not about working harder; it's about working smarter." She also said, "Garrain, I don't personally know anyone who gives as much as you do, but my question for you is, when will you start receiving at the same capacity that you give?" Mind blown!

The next day I spoke at a leadership conference, and a lady approached me with tears in her eyes. She said, "You are anointed! And I need to sow something in you right now. Will you receive it?" I saw money in her hands, and my first instinct was to tell her to put it away. Then I flashed back to the thought of me receiving at the capacity that I give, and I graciously received the money she sowed into me.

I realized that when I hadn't allowed myself to receive from others, I actually blocked their blessings. This blocked divine nature from flowing.

The bottom line is if there are areas in your life where you are lacking, dissatisfied with the outcome, or want to amplify your results, you now have a focal point that can guide you in a way that will bring your life in flow. My main focus is increasing joy in the world and being open to recieve at the capacity that I give.

The more we each express our gifts and dreams, the more they get amplified in the rhythm of nature and things begin to shift. Energy begins to move from negativity to positivity. Are you going to do what everyone else does, or are you going to be bold and courageous enough to follow your heart's calling and flow with the rhythm of nature?

EXERCISE:

1. Think of everyone you came in contact with today and practice building them up in your mind. Give them your highest regards and abundant thoughts.

2. Leave everywhere you go better than how you found it, without ever expecting anything in return. The notion of adding value from a heart that genuinely cares is the reward.

3. Whenever someone offers to support you with anything or tries to give you a gift, my suggestion is to not be so quick to turn them down. They are in the act of giving, and you just might be blocking their blessings and yours by not allowing the flow of nature to exchange between the two of you.

4. Always be intentional when saying, "thank you" or "you're welcome." It is very easy to say things when they are programmed into us. When we are intentional, it comes from a very different place. This allows us to be present and in the moment. Imagine the words *thank you* coming from a heart the size of a mountain and say it from a place of absolute gratitude. Imagine the words *you're*

welcome being received into a heart the size of a mountain.

These are very simple daily exercises that will develop the muscle of giving and receiving.

The bird is a bird and the fish is a fish. However, if the bird were to try to be a fish, could you see how life would be difficult?

The bird uses everything that it was born with, that's already inside and that alignment causes the bird to fly.

Now imagine if we as humans used everything that was already inside of us. Our version of flight is to be in flow.

What you are looking for, you already have. Alignment is the key.

CHAPTER 9

Stay in Line with the Group

*When the mind, body, and soul come together
as one, that is when we will experience our
authentic nature in flow.*

I once spoke at a leadership conference in South Africa. While I was there, I did a three-day safari in the wild, which was something I had wanted to do since I was five years old. When I arrived, I didn't know what to expect. I only knew I was overly anxious, like a kid in a candy store.

When we were given a list of instructions, I didn't care to read them or listen to anything the ranger said. It was clear that I had my own agenda. That's when Ranger Ross told me to chill and explained to me the lay of the land. "The animals out here are very dangerous. They can sense your energy. They also don't see in colors. They see shapes. So you always want to stay in line with the group. The animals are used to seeing certain shapes, so whatever changes the shape of the group poses a threat and puts all of us in danger."

I looked at him rather curiously because I had no idea what he was talking about. He basically said, "Keep the noise down, focus on gratitude, and keep all parts of your body in the truck." I thought to myself, I hear what he is saying, but I am still going to get my footage with my selfie stick. Since this was my childhood dream, I definitely displayed a childish mentality. Everything went in one ear and out the other.

When we went on the safari, I was committed to doing what I wanted to do. After several instances of being told to calm down, focus on gratitude, lower my voice, and keep my arms in the truck, the other passengers were now asking me to keep quiet. I thought, "What do these people know?" I could tell everyone was aggravated with me because of my attitude, but I didn't care.

The next day we were doing a bush walk, and I had no idea what it was at the time, so I asked Ranger Ross. He replied, "Didn't you sign off on it on the waiver?" Then I remembered I didn't even read the waiver. I just checked every box yes. Basically, I lied and told him yes, "I read it."

As Ranger Ross was giving us instructions, we were about to walk out about two miles when I said, "Hold on, aren't we supposed to go out in the truck?" Again, he said, "It's a bush walk." I said, "You got all these killer animals and one gun with six bullets. What if you use all the bullets? Then what?"

He replied, "Always focus on gratitude and whatever you do, stay in line with the group." We walked two miles from the lodge, and I was deathly afraid of even the sound of wind. The crickets sounded like dinosaurs and almost gave me a heart attack. Then there was an open field about the size of three football fields, and in the distance there was a rhinoceros walking away. I really wanted to get this footage, so I whipped out my selfie stick and slowly started to take steps to the right, away from the group. I was talking into the camera, only to be interrupted by Ranger Ross, who said, "Garrain, where are you and where are we?" When I looked up, I was about ten feet away from the group and said, "Nothing is going to happen. The rhinoceros is way over there walking in the other direction." Ranger Ross replied, "Yes, but they have a great sense of smell, and if a gust of wind bl…"

Before he could finish his sentence, a gust of wind blew, and suddenly the rhino stopped walking and turned in our direction. As the rhino was stomping its feet, Ranger Ross grabbed his rifle and said, "Garrain, lower your head, focus on gratitude, and get back in line with the group." I looked over to my right and saw a momma elephant twenty feet away, flaring her ears, staring me down, and walking in my direction. That's when I realized that being ten feet away from the group also put me in the same territory as her babies.

The times I hadn't listened flashed before my eyes, only this time, Ranger Ross was seconds away from pulling the trigger because a momma elephant and rhinoceros were threatening to charge me. My life being in danger was a confirmation. I couldn't hear anything, and it felt like my heart was beating out of my chest. Ranger Ross grabbed his gun, cocked it back, and the tone of his voice changed as he repeated in a low voice, "Garrain, lower your head, focus on gratitude, and get back in line with the group." I changed my mindset and lowered my head, focused on everything I was grateful for, which blocked out everything else, and I slowly got back in line with the group. Within 30 seconds, both animals walked away. In that moment, I was thankful that nothing happened to me and the rest of the group, and I was even more thankful that no animals were harmed due to my stubborness.

My life was changed in that moment. I now realized what alignment was. I repeated Ranger Ross's words in my mind over and over, "Stay in line with the group," and an epiphany shot through me like a cold front. I thought of all the times things went wrong in my life. My relationships, being fired from jobs, going to prison, living in my car, not being connected to my family, and most of all not being connected to myself. I realized that all these things went wrong because I was not in alignment with the highest good in my mind, body and soul. It took having my life threatened for me to embody the present moment and truly see mind, body, and soul, and it wasn't until I lowered my head and focused on gratitude. Gratitude is the glue that holds life together. Focus on gratitude and get back in line with the group, where there was protection and covering. There was favor.

Now, everytime I feel off in my life, I get to check in with myself and evaluate what's going on in my mind to see if it's in alignment with the highest good. I keep my head down which is a nod of humility and I powerfully choose to be grateful for where I am and what I have. I practice self-care, personal development, and I pray and express an extreme amount of gratitude. I share everything that I'm grateful for, like the day I came face to face with those animals in the safari.

It is in these moments where I am able to truly see and feel my authentic self at its core. I can see when and where things aren't working in my life and Boom! Get back in line with the group.

That safari really impacted me. I felt God confirmed to me the consequences of not living in alignment. I thought back to times when I was the most lost and broken, and every one of those moments was when I was out of alignment either mentally, emotionally, physically or spiritually. The times when everything was going great were when all those parts were focused and a priority. I was praying and meditating every day. I was consistent with my exercise and reading. Oddly enough, that's when things were flowing in my life, even when I wasn't aware of what I was doing.

Consider the mind, body, and soul like a three-part harmony. If even one note is sung off key, it throws the whole song off. Or with a three-legged stool, if you knock one of those legs away, the whole stool falls.

Every day that you don't nurture your alignment, it puts you at risk of continuous breakdown. "Stay in the line with the group." When the mind body and soul are activated simultaneously, it's what I like to call *the flow*.

Let's look at nature for a moment. Consider that nature is God's tempo, and in nature there is a rhythm and flow to everything. There is a calm and peacefulness to this flow. Therefore when we are in nature/alignment, we are in God's tempo. In nature, things work. Nature is in flow. It doesn't work against itself; it is in alignment with itself.

Take a fish, for example. A fish doesn't question how to swim or if it should be a fish; it uses everything that is already inside of it to be in flow with its environment.

If the fish tried to be a bird, there could be many challenges. The fish would have to learn how to breathe out of water, it would need wings so it could fly, and it would need to learn how to build a nest. The more you consider this, the more ridiculous it gets. It would be out of rhythm with its true nature. You can see how unimaginable this would be, but this is what many humans do. They try to be something they are not and wonder why their life is so difficult.

Hopefully, you're not trying to be a bird or a fish, but if you really start to listen to the things you tell yourself about what you should do, what you should have accomplished by now, or how your money, house, job, or relationships should be like someone else's, you might start to see just how much you are going against the flow of nature and your life's path. You're trying to be like a fish that wishes it was a bird.

Our purpose here on earth is to live out the fullest expression of ourselves, utilizing everything that is already inside us.

By seeing where you are out of alignment with your mind, body, and soul, you can work on building a routine or practice that supports the Group.

EXERCISE:

The Group = Mind, Body, and Soul

Take a moment to evaluate yourself. If you have not yet created a practice for being in alignment with The Group, write down a few methods that you would like to start exploring so you can connect to The Group (Mind, Body, Soul). For some of you, there may be multiple ways that you connect to The Group. The key is to discover whatever method that elevates you and taps into your operating system. When mind, body, and soul are activated simultaneously, this is what creates alignment, which is what is needed for things to flow.

Mind:

How do you intentionally grow your mind? What do you do to process a big decision, or what practices do you have that keep you calm in the busyness of life? Some examples may be meditation, journaling, reading, or finding ways to learn something new.

List 3 ways that you grow your mind and stay connected to what matters to you most.

1.
2.
3.

Body:

How do you feel most connected to your body? For some people, its working out, going for a walk in nature or playing outside with your children.

List 3 ways in which you feel your best, and your body is working at its optimum.

1.
2.
3.

Soul:

How do you feel the most connected to your soul? For some of you, its through prayer, meditation, breathing exercises, intentional silence.

List 3 ways you feel most connected to your soul.

1.
2.
3.

Once you've identified the methods that connect you to The Group, now you will have a Homebase. Whenever you feel off, or you are in breakdown, you will have Homebase to look to to see what's missing. From there, you can get back in line with The Group. It's essential to build these methods that target The Group into daily rituals. Through consistency of implementation, you will start to notice a shift in your energy, focus, and willpower. Being in alignment is Homebase. That is staying in line with The Group, so don't change the shape of the group. What you just learned about The Group and how to activate them is a very powerful tool that will support you through any situation in life. Just make sure to stay in line with The Group.

Are you still waiting to do what you said you were going to do years ago?

"You were born looking like your mom and dad but you will die looking like your decisions.

Don't be a casualty of indecision.

START NOW

Change your mindset Change your life."

Year of **CHANGE**

Sun	Mon	Tues	Wed	Thur	Fri	Sat
Now	Now	Now	Now	Now	Now	Now
Now	Now	Now	Now	Now	Now	Now
Now	Now	Now	Now	Now	Now	Now
Now	Now	Now	Now	Now	Now	Now
Now	Now	Now	Now	Now	Now	Now

There are no calendars in heaven.
START NOW because someday will
never happen.

Happy
NOW
Year

CONCLUSION

Happy NOW Year

There are no calendars in heaven,
all we have is right now.

ll you have is today—right now. There are no calendars in heaven. Whatever it is that you're designed to do, whatever it is that you feel in your heart, don't wait until tomorrow, because tomorrow may never come. Do it now and allow us to experience you at your fullest expression.

One specific experience reminded me how important this advice was when my grandmother was dying in the hospital. I had just arrived at my mom's house in Houston, and we were talking. I asked her how she was doing, and she replied, "I just don't want Momma to be in pain anymore." She said that they moved her to a hospice and that it would be time any day now.

I originally was supposed to visit Big Momma in the hospital later, but something deep inside said I needed to go earlier, so I instantly announced, "I'm going tomorrow! I just need to get there to say my peace and kiss her on the head, and then I'm going to come back."

I was already aware of how bad it had been storming and flooding all month, but I was adamant that I was going to go anyway. I woke up to several texts telling me that it wasn't a good idea to drive down there because the weather was so bad, and the flood had already killed a few people. I kept saying, "NOW is the time." The flood was almost as high as the wheels, which meant instead of six hours, it would take almost double the time, but there was this burning sensation inside and my intuition kept telling me to *go now, go now, go now.*

My friend, Gabriela, and I rented a car and drove through the swaying trees, broken branches, floods, and darkness. My stomach was burning like something inside was trying to get my attention, and the burning increased as we got closer to our destination.

Almost 10 hours later as we approached Texarkana, Texas, I saw a light in the distance. Keeping my foot on the gas, we moved forward and saw that the light was actually the sun poking through the dark clouds. The closer we got to the hospital, the brighter the light, and as soon as we parked and got out of the car, I looked up in amazement. There were dark clouds all around the hospital. The weirdest thing was that the sun was beaming right over the hospital, as if the sun's beams parted the clouds according to the certainty and faith I had in following my intuition. "Go now! Go now! Go now!"

That's when it struck me. No matter the weather, the sun is always shining brightly. Even when there are thunderstorms and dark clouds, the sun is still shining bright; it's just behind what has to pass through.

We are the ones who change our attitudes according to the weather, but if we just focus and realize that the sun is always out, there will always be beams of light, happiness, and warmth that reflect over us.

I followed my intuition and passed through darkness to reach the light where my Big Momma was waiting for me. Though she couldn't physically speak, our souls connected and communicated. I kissed her on the head, acknowledging her for everything she had ever done for everyone. I said,

"We've got it from here, Big Momma."

She somehow miraculously cracked a subtle smile. I left and Big Momma became infinite light at 5:00 a.m. that morning. My uncle told me she was waiting for me, and I cried from absolute gratitude. I had every reason in the world not to go *now*, and that experience would've never happened. I trusted, acted, followed through, and the rest was taken care of.

Where in your life are you putting things off until some other time? How many opportunities have you missed out on because you were waiting for someday to happen? When are you going to put that idea out? When are you going to write that book? When are you going to ask her out? When are you going to truly forgive him? When are you going to let go of that addiction? When will your health be the main priority in your life? When will you quit that job you can't stand that is stripping your life away and paying you less than your value? When will you leave that relationship that you don't really want to be in but you stay because they treat you better than you treat yourself? When will you realize that you deserve to be happy? When will you discover that the only person who can make you happy is YOU?

I'm assuming you are starting to see what someday is costing you in your life. Even with New Year's, people wait until January 1st to start making declarations that they literally can make right now. What exactly does "This year is my year" mean, especially when it's the same as last year with the same results? Something gets to change. All we have is right NOW, so Happy NOW Year!

Thank You

Closing Thoughts

I acknowledge you for the miracle that you are. Now you get to acknowledge yourself and the life you are meant to live. Then give it the urgency it deserves. Tomorrow is not guaranteed, so don't delay your remarkable transformation. You get to remember. Remember who you really are at the core. It's time to rediscover the inner child within you and be your amazing authentic self.

Let your light shine brightly just as it was intended to do. It's in there, inside of you, where it's always been. Do it for you. Do it for the world. Do it now.

I would like to thank you for allowing me to join you for this entire experience. The journey is life. If you truly absorbed this message and the spirit in which this book was written, you are no longer the same person you were before you picked it up and I congratulate you for playing full out.

Now, my friend, it is time to introduce your new self to the world, starting with your own reflection. Walk over to the mirror, take three slow deep breaths in your nose and out your mouth and look at that powerful, dynamic being that is full of love and hope staring back at you.

Say 100 things out loud that you are grateful for. When you are done, look at the cover of this book and truly embrace the title, *Change Your Mindset, Change Your Life*. Think about how the message in this book gave you a new perspective on how you can change your own life. That is your power.

Recall all the new levels of awareness, the breakthroughs, breakdowns, releases, and the things that were attracted to your life and feel that feeling inside your body.

Now with that emotion, take a selfie, post it on social media and introduce people to the new you—the real, authentic you. Share this book's message with them. Share what you learned, what you applied, and your newfound results. You are now on your way to achieving greater things. This is only the beginning to so much more. You are loved. I am proud of you. I acknowledge you. You are worthy, you are special, you are important, you matter, and you are everything that is associated with greatness. I could invest ten more chapters, sharing how I feel about you, but what is most important is how you feel about yourself.

So rise up, King. Rise up, Queen, and let's step into who we were meant to be and get the most of what life has to offer for us. Change Your Mindset, Change Your Life.

About the Author

Garrain Jones is a transformation coach and a globally recognized speaker. After overcoming homelessness and a life of hardships, he inspires others to lead amazing lives full of abundance. He speaks to audiences globally on the power of transformational change.

To hire Garrain Jones to keynote your next event or facilitate a workshop, go to www.GarrainJones.com/hire

Made in the USA
San Bernardino, CA
30 July 2020